Feeling VERY Much Better

D0064564

First published in 1991 by
Sally Milner Publishing Pty Ltd
17 Wharf Road
Birchgrove NSW 2041 Australia
Reprinted 1991
© Eve Campanelli 1991

Production by Sylvana Scannapiego,
Island Graphics
Design and illustrations by Doric Order
Author photograph by Eleanor Kaufman
Typeset in Australia by Asset Typesetting Pty Ltd
Printed in Australia by the Book Printer

National Library of Australia
Cataloguing-in-Publication data:

Campanelli, Eve,
    Feeling very much better.

    ISBN 1 86351 032 X

    1. Health. 2. Nutrition – Popular works. 3 Herbs –
    Therapeutic use – Popular works. 4. Attitude
    (Psychology). I. Title. (Series: Milner healthy
    living guide).

613

All rights reserved. No part of this publication may be
reproduced, stored in a retrieval system or transmitted in
any form or by any means, electronic, mechanical,
photocopying, recording or otherwise, without prior
written permission of the copyright holders.

Distributed in Australia by Transworld Publishers

Cover
Thea Proctor
Australia 1879–1966
The game. 1926
woodcut, hand-coloured on paper
15.3 x 15.0 cm
Collection: Australian National Gallery, Canberra

Feeling VERY Much Better

NUTRITION, HERBS AND A
POSITIVE ATTITUDE TO HEALTH

EVE CAMPANELLI, PhD

SALLY MILNER PUBLISHING

Preface

This book will meet the health needs of those engaged in a competitive, fast paced life, who seek a rapid yet safe and effective way to improve their health and prevent disease.

Feeling Very Much Better suggests ways to use and enjoy food and herbs to overcome many problems such as PMT, chronic colds, and other ailments, or for a general tune-up.

Most important, this book is for those who want to take charge of their own health care, who want to cut through the dizzying array of alternatives, the dozens of dos and don'ts and differing opinions.

Feeling Very Much Better contains nothing unsafe. It has no negative side effects. I am concerned with the health of the whole person, the CAUSES as well as the SYMPTOMS. I want to help people achieve and maintain optimum health through simple, natural methods that integrate body, mind and spirit, using whole foods nutrition, herbal supplements and folk remedies.

Feeling Very Much Better outlines a daily routine targeted at the healing and health maintenance of specific organ systems. For example, if acne or other skin afflictions are the problem, it will refer you to the liver cleansing and strengthening section of this book as this organ is usually the main culprit in the problem of acne. Helping the liver, in turn, will have many beneficial side effects, such as increased energy and higher spirits.

You can select one or all of the healing methods — specific foods, herbs, physical, mental and spiritual exercises — to focus on your particular condition. If you are seeking health maintenance and disease prevention, this has its own chapter, and various methods to choose from for daily life.

The information and advice in this book is not meant as a substitute for orthodox health care. While modern medical practice, with its traditional illness-orientated philosophy often fails in its mission, sometimes causing more harm than good, this book does not advocate avoidance of physicians. I am grateful to several excellent physicians in America and Europe for crisis intervention. *Feeling Very Much Better* can serve in a complementary capacity, as companion, not competitor, to modern medicine.

THIS APPROACH WORKS. Individually, the methods in this book have helped millions of people worldwide. Nutrition, herbal remedies, positive thinking and meditation have been used for centuries. Herbs were given to us for healing ourselves, and sustaining mental and spiritual health and are unsurpassed for that purpose. Modern scientific investigations into their health benefits continue to confirm their effectiveness. Medicinal herbs, the original pharmacopoeia, are now a top priority for American National Cancer Institute researchers. More than fifty-five herbs are currently under review for their therapeutic potential. The herbs listed in this book are safe, healing, nutritious and rejuvenating.

Contents

Each chapter contains a health program for a particular area of the body. It includes special foods for that area, a shopping list, foods to avoid, a one week sample menu, recommended herbs and suggestions for physical and mental exercise.

When the heart, and circulation, is functioning optimally, it will not only improve the rate of exercise and lower cholesterol, but also cure symptoms like cold hands and feet, help with chest pains, heart palpitations and trembling, insomnia, breathlessness, edema, bluish purple lips, spontaneous and/or nocturnal sweating, discomfort along the arm, high blood pressure, and blurred vision. The suggestions in this chapter will help if cardiovascular problems run in your family. Regular check-ups will confirm this. However, with advanced symptoms, undertake these techniques with your physician's supervision.

This section contains a non-mucus forming, allergy food-free diet. Apart from relieving the most common allergy symptoms like sneezing, postnasal drip and coughing, it can also help to relieve chest congestion, claustrophobia, chest distention, colds, flu, asthma, breathlessness, loss of voice, shoulder and upper backache. If you are drug dependant due to asthma, ask your physician to supervise the lowering of dosages during this program.

The kidneys extract waste from the blood, so healing the kidneys will also have other beneficial side effects like easing aching bones, reducing gas and oversensitivity to cold, overcoming low energy, dizziness, cystitis, mid to low back pain, anaemia, irregular menstruation, leaking semen, painful soles of feet, urinary incontinence, headaches, intermittent fever, sciatica, lumbago, tight calves and general back pain.

6. Strengthening and Detoxifying the Liver and Gallbladder

The liver and gallbladder work very closely together, so the information in this chapter helps them both. For instance: with the inability to digest fat, gravel or stones can form in the gallbladder, and pain below the right ribs, eczema, psoriasis, boils, acne, bruises, arthritis, depression, eye weakness, indigestion, nausea, excessive temper, menstrual problems, gout, etc., can occur. Taking care of these organs will usually be rewarded with renewed energy, wonderful skin and a new sense of well-being.

7. The Reproductive Organs and Hormonal System

Problems in this area are often also connected with liver imbalances, so pooling the information from both this and the last chapter will be doubly helpful, especially to aid exhaustion or chronic fatigue, slow metabolism, mood swings, adrenal and thyroid function, immune function, irritability, irregular menstruation, PMT, including depression, headaches, uncontrollable crying and fears, cramps, edema, menopause difficulties, prostate problems, infertility and sex drive imbalances (lacking or excessive).

8. Hypoglycemia and Diabetes 59 and the Pancreas

This chapter is for prevention and the cessation of the symptoms of hypoglycemia. It could prevent already existing diabetes from further advance and in some cases may be helpful in reducing doses of insulin. This should be monitored by your physician. The following are warning signs you can use to motivate you into prevention as outlined in this chapter: depression, irritability, blank mind, impending sense of doom, increasing blood pressure, asthma, acne, exhaustion, bloating, headaches, dizziness, allergies, excessive perspiration, blurred vision, lack of energy, prone to accidents, candida, overweight, schizophrenia.

9. For the Pregnant and 66 Nursing Woman

This chapter provides plenty of the extra nutrients required during pregnancy and nursing. Its food plan and herbal supplements are known to be especially beneficial to women at this time. Following this chapter will help prevent edema, exhaustion, nausea, toxemia, varicose veins, stretch marks, bleeding gums, 'losing a tooth', pregnancy rashes, yeast infections and premature labour.

Prevention is still the best medicine. This chapter suggests how you can stay on top now that you are back to feeling good. Perhaps you are one of the lucky ones who have never been sick but would like to experience feeling really good, rather than just not sick. The guidelines in this chapter are commonsense, good health information without making it too difficult to live our lives in the fast lane. Here's cheers to abundance in longevity, health and beauty. We can have it all.

CHAPTER 1

Introduction

A Personal Story

I had just passed my twenty-sixth birthday, and was experiencing the culture shock of recently settling in the US. A few days after my first gynaecological check up, a call came: some abnormal cells have been found, which either means that there is some kind of infection, or some malignant tissue. It's very common, don't worry about it. Check in to the hospital for a D & C on Thursday at 7 a.m.; we do dozens of these a day.

A few days after undergoing one of those 'dozens', I sat opposite the doctor in his office, and stared, quite transfixed, at his rather bad hair transplant. He told me that he had found cancer in my uterus, and that he had gone to some trouble to set time aside to perform a hysterectomy the next week. Since it was urgent, he had managed it.

My horror astounded him. 'You won't have to worry about periods any more, and God knows you don't want any children, since your boyfriend already has five'. I asked him what that had to do with me, but he didn't hear. He also told me I was probably 'cancer prone' because of a tumour which had been removed from my thigh a year ago.

I consulted other doctors and each, 'the best in his field', offered the same opinion: cancer of the cervix and uterus. I decided not to have a hysterectomy. On hearing this, most of my friends and relatives were agitated, to put it mildly, and the first gynaecologist's hair definitely stood up on end at my decision. Actually, I felt quite calm. I signed a release saying I had refused treatment, and promised to come back three months later.

At that follow-up visit he cleared his throat and said, 'we found no malignancy with this test — these things happen sometimes, we must have got it all the first time'.

That decision, dear reader, was not a frivolous one. I had simply had enough of being a victim, and was ready to take some responsibility for my illnesses. Since I saw my role in creating my illness, surely I could 'uncreate' it. But how, and what to do?

During those three months I read everything I could get my hands on regarding alternative health treatments, and realised that many unnecessary hysterectomies are performed. I was impressed by the fact that not only had many of the alternative treatments existed well before modern medicine, they are generally non-toxic, and therefore, have no bad side effects.

I had watched my mother suffer horrendous migraines, my first husband died of cancer (he was a chain smoker), I had suffered from chronic cystitis since childhood. At twenty-five part of my thigh was removed due to a malignancy; at twenty-six the D & C was to cost me three late miscarriages in as many years.

When being ill on a regular basis first began, there was something wonderful about it. I felt protected and taken care of. It was like time out with no guilt. There were flowers and caring visits from friends. The only problem was, that once the novelty wore off, I got bedsores instead of flowers and friends became otherwise engaged. That gave me plenty of time to think. What was I getting out of this? Did I still need it? If not, what would I do about it? How much of my life would I have to change? Was I doing anything that was positive? If so how could I build on that?

At thirty, I decided to become a serious student of alternative health care methods. The three happiest, busiest years of my life followed: sixteen hour days, seven days a week of work and study and I had my bachelor's degree. The years of illness and soul searching were a great gift — easy to say in hindsight, isn't it? They gave me a life and a career about to happen, that I loved. For the first time I felt healthy, strong and had found my niche.

It seems things are not so laborious when we are on the right track. Instead of having to worry about how I would make a living, my first client approached me during chemistry class. Did I know what to do about cystitis (bladder infection)? Did I know? Not only did I know but I had first hand experience, I could certainly sympathise. She had taken all kinds of medication for years and it kept coming back. We set up a time for the next day. Her diet was too acidic, she drank very little water and always wore tight pants and often nylon underwear. I worked with her with the remedies in this book (see kidney/bladder section). Her infection caused no more pain in twenty-four hours and in three days was cleared up completely. She always keeps some Uva Ursi and water handy now.

This woman sent many others. One, with chronic headaches which occurred especially in the mid afternoon, ate a lunch that contained only tiny amounts of food along with the chemicals! Her cardboard hamburger had some lettuce with it, sprayed with a preserving chemical, but nevertheless it contained some roughage. Dessert was ice cream made mostly from dye and gasoline. Acne and fatigue were also revealed during our talk. She could probably have helped herself by just eating some living foods once in a while, but she wanted a change quickly. We used yellow dock and boldo leaves along with her new diet to appease and assist her unhappy liver. Her headaches were worse for the next two days and suddenly totally gone by the third. (You know the old saying, sometimes it has to get worse before it gets better.) Her acne had cleared in a week and she reported feeling much better.

Some particular challenges in those early days were men who were 'only here because my wife insisted'. One example was a male nurse — big — forty-five years old. His bronchial asthma was so severe that he only slept two hours at a time before needing to take one or more of four different debilitating medications. Sitting opposite me, he crossed his arms and legs, and dared me to attempt on him all this quackery he had heard about. A week later he slept through each night using no medication, and was back at work. Since his condition was so extreme and he clearly wanted results yesterday, I suggested a strict allergy diet, bowel cleansers and plenty of nourishing juices to cleanse and soothe his body. I gave him herb blends including juniper and cubeb berries, comfrey and watercress. These help rid the body of mucus. (See allergies in the respiratory system section.)

A twenty-six-year-old man took two pain tablets each meal for daily digestive upsets, painful sinuses, and again, headaches, exhaustion and acne. It took two weeks to get down to one pain pill a day, and he was symptom-free. Apple cider vinegar, aloe, garlic, horsetail and cascara sagrada were some of the herbs we used. (See liver and detoxification chapters). He also found a girlfriend and an enjoyable job when he felt better. The universe is generous when we do our part — well, most of the time anyway.

There are many similar case histories in this book. Some are used in the different chapters to give you inspiration and support in your own decision to begin feeling much better.

By the time I was thirty-five my practice was thriving. I was grateful, happy and still symptom-free. That year I met my present husband and began my PhD in Holistic Health at Ryokan College in Los Angeles.

Word of mouth, which is the best source of new clients, got around to the various film studios in Los Angeles, and before long I was seeing many members of crews and casts.

At first, I had to deal with my own stage fright when I was consulted by George Hamilton, Lily Tomlin, Morgan Fairchild and others. Most were delightful and fun to work with. When Lily asked me to work with her mother who is also very funny, I was thrilled. I knew now that I really could contribute to life rather than fearfully retreat from its challenges by being ill. We all have special gifts to give and a need to keep growing until we find what they are, is part of healing ourselves.

Of course, it doesn't stop there (wouldn't you know it) just when we think it is safe. By thirty-seven I had completed my PhD and at thirty-nine, against all the odds, I was delivered of a bonnie wee boy.

Perhaps you have some reasons for change at this point in your life which happily coincide with the ideas in this book. I know it will make your own road to well being and fitness more fun and shorter — in keeping with 'Life in the Fast Lane''.

Herbs — The Perfect Nourishing and Healing Supplement to our Diets

Hippocrates, sometimes called the father of modern medicine, was the first of the Greek physicians to concern himself with healing as a logical science. Significantly, Hippocrates considered medical practice and herbalism to be synonymous. Most of his healing substances were derived from plants, and included such common herbs as rosemary, vervain, mint and sage. Unlike his predecessors, Hippocrates approached the use of plant medicines empirically and systematically, successfully divorcing magic and demonology from contemporary philosophies of herbalism. He left a list of 400 herbal cures — fewer than the enormous compilations of the eastern civilisations, but important as a cornerstone of subsequent European plant knowledge.

Further back in time than that, the earliest known book devoted solely to medicinal plants was the pharmacopoeia of the Emperor Shen Nung, called the *Pen Tsao*. This document is dated 3000 BC, and describes 365 curing herbs, including ma-huang, the shrub from which modern medicine derived ephedrine, a potent lung dilator, currently used in the treatment of asthma.

Though this is the earliest written text known, the science of herbology has its roots at the dawn of civilisation — and before. Excavations of 60 000 year old Neanderthal burial grounds at Shanidar in Iraq reveal that the dead were covered with plants still found in modern herbal pharmacopoeias, including yarrow, groundsel, hollyhock, grape hyacinth, thistle and ephedra.

There are also many biblical references to herbs

given us for food and medicine.

Herbs are the perfect 'vitamins', produced by the wisdom of the universe. It is evident that the nutrients stored within the plants' cellular structures are in forms that are easily metabolised by the gastric juices, enzymes and hormones of the body. Herbs contain minerals, vitamins and salts that help strengthen the body's resistance, strengthen tissues and improve the nervous system. They also contain glycosides which are important sugars for the proper functioning of the heart and bloodstream. Plant mucilage can assist in the proper functioning of the intestines. Tannins present in herbs aid in preventing harmful bacteria.

To receive the most beneficial effects from herbs, they should be consumed regularly over long periods of time. They should be kept in airtight containers away from heat, light and dampness. Do not refrigerate. Also important is the quality and care they receive en-route to you. Local suppliers are easiest to question, and, of course, the efficacy of the herbs will make itself known to you in short order. Your herbalist or health food store should also be able to recommend the best.

The preparations which stand up well to long-term storage and use are the dried encapsulated herbs and those prepared with alcohol, apple cider vinegar or oils, as in tinctures or ointments. The preparations of tinctures, oils, etc., are beyond the scope of this book, but are readily available in health food shops, at herbalists and some pharmacies, as are the capsules.

But one easy way to take dried herbs is as tea. *To make medicinal herb teas,* use a glass coffee pot, as herbs absorb metal. Pour in 1 litre of water and four heaping tablespoons of herbs. Bring to a boil, and let simmer on low for 10 minutes for roots; for leaves and flowers, just pour on the boiling water and let steep for 10-15 minutes, covered. Let cool and strain into a glass container. Store in the refrigerator. Take 2-4 cups a day, according to your size and the severity of your symptoms.

I like to use *herb teas as a pleasant hot beverage,* especially during the winter, adding a little honey or pure maple syrup. Peppermint tea settles my stomach after a big lunch and is readily available in restaurants or a tea bag or two can be kept in one's handbag or pocket. (It's not recommended as a good washing powder additive, however, so make sure you remove them before you throw that piece of clothing in the wash.) A cup of chamomile, vervain or linden tea is soothing at night and a nice way to get ready for bed. Most health food stores carry a large variety of herb teas in bags to experiment with. They do not have toxic side effects (or significant medicinal value) even if you drink several cups a day, as they are usually not steeped long enough. Steeping past 2-3 minutes tends to turn them bitter, which defeats the purpose of enjoying a pleasant, healthy beverage.

I have listed a sufficient number of medicinal herbs for the various symptoms in each chapter, so that if some are not available, others will be. Very occasionally you may find listed in this book a herb like comfrey or lobelia inflata which is restricted in some countries. In these cases just use the herbs listed that are available. It is a shame about these two herbs in particular as they are wonderfully effective and I have yet to see a negative side effect from them in my practice. Nor would there be any, if used in the amounts recommended in this book. I feel these restrictions are largely political.

Suggested herbs are not meant to take the place of any important medical treatment prescribed by your doctor. They are supplements which can improve your general health and address specific ailments. It is always wise to consult your physician if you are on medication and intend to change your health habits.

Nutrition for Health

Just as the car only runs well on fuels meant for it, so the body only functions well on foods that nourish it, foods that can replenish it after work, play and mental and physical stresses. Devitalised, toxic foods, will eventually produce a devitalised, toxic body. A devitalised, toxic body cannot protect itself from disease. Food is not, of course, the only culprit that allows disease into our bodies, it just plays a very large part. Pollution and the role of the mind and spirit are other factors and they are also taken into consideration throughout the health plan in this book.

The foods listed here are wholesome and well balanced. Their quality varies from state to state, country to country and season to season. The best bet is to choose the foods listed that are indigenous to your area, seasonal, fresh and organic, when possible. The effort is well rewarded with more enjoyment of your meals, and a greater sense of well-being.

If few or none of these are available, just do what you can, add a positive mental attitude and sense of humour to bridge the gaps. It's amazing how well *they* can work.

Good nutrition is not only what we eat, but also what we assimilate properly. In other words, how much our digestive system actually makes available to our body for proper upkeep. The herbs and foods in this book all aid in this process by cleansing, nourishing and restoring the body.

Remember:

Drink only enough with meals to take any supplements that should be taken at this time, as liquids dilute the digestive juices, and can cause improper digestion.

Chew your food well and slowly; proper digestion begins in the mouth.

Substitute foods that you do like for the ones that you don't, as there are plenty to choose from. Trying different ways of preparing the foods you didn't like, however, may give your taste buds a pleasant surprise.

Ask your health food store to order the foods you want. They are usually happy to do so.

Use virgin olive oil, butter, sour cream and yoghurt in moderation, and instead of artificial dairy products and margarine. Margarine, touted for its low cholesterol value, is now suspected of being a carcinogen. I usually use ripe avocados instead of butter in sandwiches.

If you are the type of person who prefers to make changes slowly, instead of doing it cold turkey, look at the 'foods to avoid' list in your section and eliminate one at a time, replacing it with the equivalent in the 'foods to eat' section.

If you eat out a lot, choose quality restaurants. Where possible, order the closest thing to your 'food plan', or know what you want before hand and ask for it. Looking at the menu may sway your resolution. If they do not have anything you want, eat the best they have and think positive.

In each section of this book you can eat all the fruits, vegetables, whole grains, nuts, seeds and legumes you want, and there are many of them. Just double check the 'foods to avoid' list for exceptions in your case.

Use meats and dairy foods sparingly, as an accessory to other foods, rather than making them the star attraction. Get the meats and poultry hormone and antibiotic-free whenever possible. Replace cow's milk products with goat's milk, soy milk, nut milk or juice. No meat or dairy food is necessary for health. The food plans in this book provide all necessary nutrients, including protein and calcium.

Replace coffee and black tea with herb teas, juices and mineral water (no gas), whenever possible.

Proper food combinations help:

> Avoid eating meat and bread at the same meal.

> Avoid eating fruit and vegetables at the same meal.

> Avoid eating more than one carbohydrate at a meal, e.g., don't eat potatoes, rice or bread together.

> Avoid eating citrus juice and grains together as they ferment in the stomach.

> Eat melon by itself.

Relax — take a breath before you eat. A tight stomach and mind can turn even healthy food into guided missiles in the body. Don't take it all too seriously, misery is a lot more destructive than occasional junk food.

There are often initial detoxification reactions — see the detoxification chapter for details.

The Role of the Mind in Changing from Disease to Health

'What the mind can conceive and enthusiastically believe, it can achieve.'
Napoleon Hill

Our minds are much more powerful than we realise. Our thoughts are power movers. Most of us have heard that 'we are what we eat'. We are also what we think. The things we fear often come to pass because we think about them so much we visualise them, we create them. One family member has a cold and you say, 'I'm bound to catch it' — sure enough, you will. 'Sally be careful you don't drop that $5000 Ming vase'. Both of you are visualising it now and sure enough, there it goes.

Instead we can focus our minds on the things we do want, whether it be health, joy, love or abundance. Visualise health where there is disease, see it breaking up and leaving the body, being replaced by healthy tissue and cells. The mind follows instructions. It may take some time and patience depending on how long the negative conditioning has gone on, but it will happen. Repeat positive affirmations to yourself whenever you have a moment. Whenever a negative thought comes up, 'I'm never going to get rid of this cough', say 'cancel, cancel, cancel', and replace it with: 'I am *now* in the process of getting better, and I give thanks. By Thursday (be specific) I see myself running around the block again.' Well, something like that. Make up phrases that sound like you.

Good times to practise affirmations and visualisations are first thing in the morning before you are fully awake — visualise waking up five minutes earlier, so you have time to do this — and before going to sleep. Of course any time is good, but at these times we have easier access to our subconscious.

Reading a few pages a day of the motivational books listed in the back of this book, especially before sleep, is always helpful. I would never have finished writing this book without them.

CHAPTER 2

A Clean Start
Food For A Week
Of Detoxification

Body signals asking for detoxification!

Digestive problems, abdominal distention, nausea, diarrhoea, constipation, gas, heartburn, shoulder pains, skin problems, excessive sensitivity to noise, dull tired eyes, overweight, underweight, nervousness, chronic fatigue.

'Detoxification' — *To remove the poison or the effects of poison from . . .*
Webster's Dictionary

Detoxifying the body is like spring cleaning it of waste and various unwanted collectibles that have been hiding in corners unknown for years, especially in our intestines. These clogging collectibles interfere with proper passage and absorption of nutrients. This in turn sends misleading signals to the hypothalamus gland, located in the brain, that says: 'feed me, feed me'. Since nutrient-free foods like white bread and sugar do not shut off this signal, we eat more and more and are still malnourished while getting fatter and more nervous and tired each day. Eliminating waste and eating nutrient-rich foods will begin to restore health, regulate the appetite and shut the signal off.

This process is an excellent way to begin dealing with disease, since the body's increased physical efficiency cannot help but affect the entire body, and in turn, the mind. PREVENTION of disease is another excellent reason to detoxify regularly, as it helps to keep the immune system strong. In the USA, one in three people suffer from cancer, one million people a year die of heart and circulatory diseases and 34 million are overweight or obese. The figures for other western societies are similar. Detoxification on an occasional or regular basis will help you to prevent becoming one of these statistics.

The word detoxification might sound pretty drastic, however, it rarely is. In fact, considering the build-up over the years of toxic by-products and poor eating habits, then detoxifying and resting it once in a while, seems the least we can do for our bodies. The benefits definitely outweigh the occasional and very temporary unpleasant side effects, showing us life in technicolour again as opposed to black and white.

There can be withdrawal symptoms from 'drug foods' such as sugar and coffee in the first 3-4 days. Typical symptoms are: headaches, irritability, gas, bloating and other digestive upsets. If headaches become too much of a problem even for a short time, try drinking extra water and make sure the bowels are moving. Outside that, get a neck rub or adjustment from your chiropractor, and *as a last resort* take a pain pill with lots of water. The diet over the next week will compensate.

You may initially lose your appetite. That's good. Don't eat. The rest will do your system good. Just drink fresh juices for your nutrients and your appetite will come back, much to your chagrin. You may feel permanently hungry, or so it may seem. That's good, too. Eat more fresh fruits and vegetables, or make a hot filling soup with them. You could also just acknowledge it to yourself as a passing phase, because that's what it is.

Before you begin, *write your goal down* on a piece of paper and look at it several times a day. It will be a gentle reminder if you are feeling 'a bit off' that your body is just throwing out what you've been throwing in all these years. 'I can't believe how good I feel', is what 95 per cent of people say after the first week.

'J' was totally frustrated with chronic constipation, headaches, psoriasis and a foul temper, the latter being a family complaint. He felt constipation was a way of life and just wanted whatever I had given his friend for psoriasis, since his friend was better now. It was clear to me he was in need of a detoxification, so I suggested that we make that decision in a week's time, since not everyone benefits from the same thing and the causes of the disease are often different. We used a herbal toner and cleanser for the intestines. This consisted mainly of cayenne pepper (also excellent for the heart and circulation), cascara sagrada, turkey rhubarb and yellow dock. Twice a day he used psyllium husks with fresh juice. (See healing herbs in this chapter.)

He followed his diet — see below — about 80 per cent of the time, he thought, and called me on his second day with an unflattering opinion of my services. A week later we had an amusing visit discussing his phone call and outlined the coming week. His psoriasis was 80 per cent better, we cut back the herbs slightly, adjusted the diet by adding a little extra virgin olive oil to his salads and kept an eye on things. He never needed the herb combination for psoriasis, just a 'house cleaning'.

Try to avoid the following reasoning for not staying on track. A client called me two days before the end of her first week detoxification appointment to say she wasn't coming in because she felt there was something wrong with the detoxification. She was feeling tired, irritable and had an upset stomach on the second day. That night she went to a party, had some cocktail type food — you know the kind — and a couple of drinks, and felt much better immediately. After all, she had come to see me because she wanted to feel better, not worse. It obviously wasn't the right time for her. She wasn't ready. She came back three months later and we tried it again and she did fine.

I think we owe it to ourselves and our purse strings to detoxify our bodies before we buy different remedies for each complaint we have. As there are usually many complaints at one time we often overmedicate. Once we are cleansed we often find we need very little, remedy-wise, to keep ourselves healthy. Simply realise that the first few days just have to be gotten through. It's a good time to pamper yourself a little. Get a massage, walk on the beach, read a good book or watch some good movies — not at the theatre though, you don't want to have to deal with the smell of popcorn and candy at the beginning. Later it's easy and even having a little break out won't set you back too much.

The following foods will allow the body a vacation from the non-foods which have overworked and underpaid your system for so long. Also do not worry about where your protein and calcium is coming from.

It is all in the foods listed, and now you will actually absorb more of it.

When you are on the detoxification diet take extra vitamin C (between 4–10 000 mg a day) according to your size and tolerance. You will know you have reached your limit when the bowels get loose. Then cut it back by 1–2000 mg until they stabilise. For further information on vitamin C, I highly recommend any of Linus Pauling's books on vitamin C. They are available at most major book and health food stores.

The following foods greatly assist the breakdown and elimination of unwanted collectibles in the body and aid digestion. All other fruits, vegetables and whole grains may be used, unless listed below under 'foods to avoid'.

Food for a Week

MAIN SHOPPING LIST ITEMS

All fruits and vegetables except those you feel you are allergic to. If you know strawberries give you a rash, don't eat them. Avoid tomatoes and products thereof, as they are high on most allergy lists.

All fresh juices or you can make your own. You'll need carrots, spinach, apples, grapefruit and grapes. Use them singly or in a blend and dilute with water.

All whole grains except wheat for the first two weeks — many people are allergic to it. Then try it for one meal and see how you feel. Avoid roasted and popped grains like popcorn at the beginning, as they are gas forming, and the extreme heat used to pop them removes most of the nutrients. Buy brown rice, millet, oatmeal, rye and buckwheat. (See the breakfast recipes.)

Substitute bread with rye crackers or rice cakes. Use

sprouted grain bread, sourdough rye, or other wheat-free bread from your health food store in moderation. 1-2 pieces a day.

Dairy foods — use only as an occasional side dish and then only if it doesn't make you 'mucousy'. You can tell if it does that, when you wake up with mucus at the back of your throat or a runny nose. Dairy foods should be raw when possible and/or soured: raw unsalted butter, raw cheese, buttermilk, yoghurt, sour cream and kefir. Otherwise use substitutes like soy, goat or rice cheeses, milks.

Meats — are best avoided during the first two weeks. If you are a true dedicated consumer, however, reduce use to 2-3 times a week as a complement to vegetable dishes, rather than making it the star attraction. Buy it hormone-free and antibiotic-free when possible. Many restaurants now use free range meats.

Other shopping list items are:

lemons	herb teas
pure water	herbs listed below
(no bubbles)	lots of leafy greens for
apple cider vinegar	salads like:
virgin olive oil	lettuce
mustard	spinach
herb seasonings	English spinach
raw unsalted nuts	swiss chard
potatoes to	cabbage
bake or steam	parsley
yams	watercress
whole grain pasta	and fresh herbs
plain yoghurt	raw nuts and/or seeds
molasses or tupelo	can be added to
honey	salads for more body
dates	(see recipes)

Eat only if you are hungry. Not everything listed below needs to be eaten. If you think you are getting a hunger signal, drink a glass of purified water first and recheck. Chew the food thoroughly, and don't eat if you are upset. That alone should keep the weight down, shouldn't it? Changes in the order of meals may be made. Don't stick to your traditional patterns. Make the soaked grains the night before starting and use them three mornings a week.

Healing Herbs

Psyllium husks and bentonite liquid, available in all health food stores, with instructions. Simply use 1-2 teaspoons of each according to your size in 120 ml (4 fl. oz) of fresh juice. First thing in the morning, shake and drink quickly before it gels. Follow with 120-180 ml (4-6 fl. oz) of pure water. This mixture takes your collectibles out with it when it leaves. However it is not laxative, so if you have even the slightest problem with constipation, buy some aloe, cascara sagrada, cayenne, turkey rhubarb, yellow dock, senna and/or wormwood singly or in an already existing herbal combination from your herbalist or health food store. These will make sure things keep moving. They will also shorten your withdrawal time. Take your first capsule at dinner the night before you start. Raise the dose if you need to, then ease off as your body lets you know.

If you have recently and/or over the years taken a lot of antibiotics, buy some acidophyllus from your health food store and take twice a day on an empty stomach for a week. This will restore the friendly bacteria in your intestine that the antibiotics have removed.

The Diet

On arising

1 glass of warm water with fresh juice of ½ lemon;

or

120 ml (4 fl. oz) fresh carrot, or fresh apple and spinach or fresh grapefruit juice. Don't use more than 1 part spinach to 3 parts carrot or apple juice. It's very laxative. Unsweetened grape juice can be made fresh or bought off the shelf.

Breakfast

Raw cottage cheese or yoghurt with fresh fruit — if dairy food doesn't cause congestion;

or

Fresh fruit in season;

or

Whole grain cereals. These are especially warming in the winter. Alternate the ones listed in the recipes under breakfast.

Mid morning

Up to 240 ml (8 fl. oz) of fresh juice with equal parts water, or a fruit or vegetable.

Lunch

Raw vegetable salad. Vary all your favourite vegetables.

Dressing: apple cider vinegar or lemon juice with virgin olive oil, mustard and fresh herbs and seasonings of your choice. One of my favourites is dill weed;

or

Vegetable soup or stew may be used instead of/or as well as salad;
or
Fruit salad with raw nuts, if you did not have it for breakfast. Use rye or rice crackers with these if you like.

Mid afternoon   Same as mid morning.

Dinner   Half hour before, drink 180 ml (6 fl. oz) pure water with one tablespoon apple cider vinegar. It's a wonderful appetite suppressor, blood cleanser and digestant.

Steamed or wok cooked vegetables with brown rice or with baked potato or yam or whole grain pasta or soup and/or salad. Meat twice a week if desired — sauté thin slices with the vegetables.

Dessert   At least one hour later: baked apple;
or
Low fat yoghurt and berries. Add molasses or honey or pure maple syrup if desired;
or
Dates and mint tea;
or
Baked pear;
or
Fresh fruit in season.
Herb tea.

FOODS AND HABITS TO AVOID

Refined sugar, flour, in fact anything refined, pasteu-rised dairy foods, meat, salt, coffee, tea, soft drinks, especially diet soft drinks, wheat, tomato products, chocolate — oh, no!

Drinking a lot of any liquids with meals, alcohol (at least for the first 2-3 weeks), 'inhaling' food as opposed to relaxing and chewing properly, combining carbohydrates like bread and potatoes with meats during this time (too hard to digest), combining vegetables with fruits (the gas that forms won't enhance social life), combining citrus fruits with grains (they ferment and make you sleepy). Eating meat containing hormones or antibiotics. Watching TV food ads.

Exercise and a Positive Mind Set

A good 'sweat up' from a cardiovascular exercise four times a week will speed the detoxification enormously. Stretches and yoga exercise are also very helpful. I go on three detoxifications per year, lasting about 10 days each, and one 10-day fresh juice or watermelon fast a year. During that time, more than any other, I really enjoy my runs, aerobic work-outs or bike rides; not necessarily during the first two days, but after that my energy is far superior to when I'm eating 'regularly'. I expect you will find this, too. The body feels much lighter. It also helps with the appetite. Drinking a glass of fresh vegetable juice and water afterwards, with a few minutes rest, stretches and positive affirmations can make for a great day.

Releasing physical garbage makes it a lot easier to let go of mental garbage as well. Pick a person each day you have a grievance against and repeat constantly during the exercise 'I now let go of my grievance against . . .' Of course, putting this in your own words is likely to make this infinitely more effective. 'I feel as if a load is lifted off me' is another good example I use a lot. Positive thinking and motivational books are great to read at this time.

CHAPTER 3

Strengthening the Cardiovascular System

Some signs of imbalance

> Cold hands and feet and other circulatory problems. Chest pain, heart palpitations, trembling, insomnia, breathlessness, edema, purple lips, spontaneous and/or nocturnal sweating, discomfort along the arm, high blood pressure and blurred vision.

The heart is the symbol of our emotions, its steady beat controls our blood vessels and the circulation of the blood. It assists in thyroid control and influences menopause, amongst many other functions. One million people die of diseases of this system each year — you don't have to be one of them, even if it does run in your family.

The area in which I consistently find my suggestions most effective is in blood pressure regulation, especially before medication is used, in cases where the physician threatens medication and/or imminent disaster 'if you don't lose weight and do something about your stress'. Committed participation in these healing suggestions produced excellent results 90 per cent of the time within about six weeks.

The following genuine case history may also help to inspire you: I had been seeing 'Mr G's' daughter for preventative health care for some years when she sent her father in to see me. They had always had a close relationship and one could see why. He had a great sense of humour and loved life. At that time, however, he was frustrated and disillusioned with what had been happening to his body of late. He trusted his daughter's suggestion to investigate alternative health care.

His physician had diagnosed high blood pressure and appropriate medication. It cramped his style because, since he had been taking it, he experienced low energy, depression and he had become impotent. His wife was equally upset and worried about him. They had a long and happy marriage, both being in their late fifties. He lived in New York where the medication had been prescribed and was visiting his daughter in Los Angeles. His Los Angeles physician thought the herb and diet program I suggested was a great idea and, at least, could do no harm. He monitored his progress, reducing his medication as his blood pressure came down. After six weeks it was within the high range of normal, his medication was minimal and to his and his wife's joy his libido was back to normal. Another reminder that traditional and preventative medicine need not be in conflict.

You may be experiencing one or more of these symptoms or you may have just been told your cholesterol is too high. In any of these cases the following suggestions will be helpful.

Heart Herbs

These herbs are historically known to soften hardened arteries, encourage proper circulation, clean out plaque, lower cholesterol and strengthen the heart.

Psyllium husks, when mixed in juice and used on arising soften stools, cleanse and improve elimination of waste and toxins. A clean digestive system is essential for proper absorption and assimilation of the other heart herbs and foods.

Borage, hawthorne, capsicum, (cayenne), motherwort and garlic, are not only excellent heart herbs, but garlic also keeps the vampires away. Borage was also touted by Nicholas Culpepper, the famous British herbalist, as one for those who suffered from 'often swoonings' of the heart. It also makes a delicious tea. They can be used singly, or in combinations of two, three or more. They are available in health food stores or check the list of mail order suppliers in the back of this book.

Start with one capsule of the dried, powdered herbs per day, with meals, and gradually work your way up to between 4-8 per day, according to your size. If capsules are unavailable and/or you can't swallow them anyway, the tinctures are just as good and available from health food stores or health care practitioners.

MAIN SHOPPING LIST ITEMS
Millet, buckwheat, oats, sunflower seeds, sesame seeds, ripe bananas, potatoes, okra, shitake mushrooms, sea vegetables, apples, raw honey, cold pressed virgin oil, whole grains, molasses, apricots, grapes, red beets and fresh oysters. Also use all other fruits and vegetables except those listed below under foods to avoid.

Also, artichokes, lemons, pure water, carrots, celery,

parsley, spinach, psyllium husks, dried apricots, apples, whole grain bread, miso soup available in instant soup form, lots of yellow and orange vegetables like carrots, banana, cabbage, summer squash, broccoli, kale, collards, brussels sprouts, yams, sweet potatoes, brown rice or basmati rice. Wakame or other sea vegetables are available, dried, at your healthfood store. When going to a Japanese restaurant, try their fresh seaweed salads — delicious. Plain yoghurt, berries, mint tea and other herb teas. Borage and linden tea are two of my favourites. Also vervain, which is served in the brasseries in France as commonly as coffee, its antithesis.

These foods are especially beneficial to the heart and will help to lower high serum cholesterol levels and free up the arteries. However, ALL fruits, vegetables, whole grains, may be used except those listed under 'foods to avoid'. Health food stores will assist you with all the items you are not familiar with, and will usually order goods in for you if they don't have them.

If you eat out a lot, go to Japanese and health oriented restaurants more often. They will have a lot of these foods. Many fine restaurants will serve you any steamed vegetables you want or an artichoke, or pasta with garlic and olive oil, or baked potatoes. Vegetarian Mexican restaurants are good, too.

The Diet

ONE WEEK SAMPLE MENU FOR THE HEART

On arising   Squeeze the juice of ½ lemon into a glass of pure water, or juice the following combination: carrot, celery, parsley and spinach. Dilute with ½ water. Drink about 120 ml

(4 fl. oz) now with psyllium husks, (shake and drink quickly as they swell), and the rest during the day.

If you don't have a juicer, buy a fresh juice combination close to this at your health food store.

Breakfast

Millet (used in European health spas for heart and diabetes problems), three times a week. See recipes.

Buckwheat twice a week. Oatmeal once a week. (See recipes for all these grains.) Just fruit for breakfast, including ripe bananas, is just as good. If you are not hungry now, don't eat. The juice will last you a while, then eat when you feel hungry.

Mid morning

1-2 ripe bananas, or a handful of dried apricots or apples or a bunch of grapes.

Lunch

A large, raw vegetable salad with an olive oil and lemon juice or apple cider vinegar dressing, with a piece of whole grain bread. If you have trouble digesting raw vegetable salads, vegetable soup is the next best (see recipes). Gradually, as your digestion improves, start with small salads and build up.

Mid afternoon

Same as mid morning.

Dinner

Miso soup and steamed or sautéed vegetables, especially yellow and orange vegetables such as carrots, banana squash, cabbage, summer squash, broccoli, kale, collards and brussels sprouts with basmati or brown rice. All root vegetables are good;

or

Different soups, using these and other vegetables adding shitake mushrooms and wakame or other sea vegetables (especially good for high cholesterol). Add salad any time.

Dessert At least 1 hour later. Low fat plain yoghurt with berries and raw honey;

or

Dates and mint tea;

or

Baked apple;

or

Fresh fruit.

FOODS TO AVOID

The 'tough' part — all refined foods (foods that used to be brown and are now white). Salty foods (cause bloating), pasteurised dairy products (indigestible, make mucus, cause allergies), additives and preservatives (liver distress and possible carcinogens). Red meat, coffee, black tea, soft drinks, sugar, spicy and fried foods. Become a label reader, you may need your glasses for the small print.

Note: Since it is now acknowledged that a large consumption of meat is a major cause of heart disease, it is best avoided until good health is restored, and then used in moderation. The 'addict', however, might cut back to three to four times a week, using hormone-free, antibiotic-free meat whenever possible. Grill instead of fry, undercook it, and eat it with plenty of fresh vegetables instead of bread or potatoes.

Exercises for the Body-Mind-Spirit and Heart

These can be done any time of the day, however, they do help to wake you up in the morning.

1. Take a few sips of diluted juice to pick up the blood sugar and take it with you to your stretching area to sip on.

2. While stretching, keep your mind clear of problems by listening to something that makes you laugh or imagine something that might. Laughter is the very best exercise for the heart (see Norman Cousin's book *Anatomy of an illness*).

3. As the mind becomes distracted again, repeat mentally 'I know my problems are learning experiences — I choose to see things peacefully today'. Try it, it feels good, and you don't have to tell anybody!

4. Start a yoga class — your heart will love you for it, or just begin with these minimal exercises at home
   a. Feet 30 cm (12″) apart, reach for the sky, exhaling with each reach, alternating arms up to 12 times each side.
   b. Gently pull head to left knee, then right, three times each side, exhaling each pull.

c. Feet still 30 cm (12″) apart, from waist up only, swing arms loosely from side to side.

d. Bring legs into a stride position. Bend front leg to a right angle, keeping back leg as straight as possible. Raise arms overhead, hold for a few seconds. Straighten front leg, pull head down to front leg and repeat on other side, three times each. Just do as much as you comfortably can and remember the affirmations. ALL STRETCHES three minutes in total.

5. Cardiovascular exercise is most important for the heart, at least three times a week. Two of those times could be on the weekend. Some choices are: walking, speed walking, swimming, jogging, aerobics, biking (stationery or free). Check with your health care practitioner. Build up slowly to at least 20 minutes.

Heart problems are sometimes known to be caused by a lack of compassion for one's self. Naw — impossible!

6. Simply meditating — best after exercise, but good anytime. Take from three minutes up to as long as you want.

a. Sit up cross legged or in chair with back straight, chin tucked slightly in.

b. As you inhale deeply, yet easily into the belly, imagine energy from the universe going into the top of the head, down to the base of the spine. Keep the shoulders relaxed. On the exhale, see the breath going back up and out into the most peaceful scene you can imagine, e.g. a starry sky, a stream in a field.

c. In the shower. This is a great place to do this sound exercise for the heart, because, (1) nobody can hear you, and (2) the steam helps to clear out the breathing passages. Clasp the hands behind the neck, straightening up and on the exhale, from the bottom of the diaphragm, loudly say HAAAH. Take another breath, repeat eight times. Takes one minute, and feels good.

Using all of these 'strengthening the heart' practices would be ideal in speeding your progress, however, just do what time permits so it doesn't become an added stress. Choose one or two to begin with — just the herbs, or just the meditation, and you will feel better. Enjoy — and here's to a happy heart!

CHAPTER 4

The Respiratory
System

A mucusless, allergy-free diet

Some signs of imbalance

> Problems in any part of this system are not
> necessarily only indicated by allergies as we
> commonly know them, but also colds, 'flu,
> coughs, asthma, bronchitis, sneezing, laryngitis,
> and sinusitis, claustrophobia, loss of voice, aches
> in the upper back and shoulders, fatigue, and
> skin and hair problems.

Food allergies are often a side effect of a lowered
immune function. The suggestions in this chapter will
help with that, as will the 'liver and gallbladder'
chapter. Using the herbal recommendations from both
chapters, will speed your progress.

The popular theory 'I know what my body needs
because I crave for certain foods', does not hold water,
so to speak, until we are perfectly healthy. Before that,
we actually crave the foods we are allergic to. Just like
a heroin addict craves heroin. That it's beneficial,
however, is dubious. The suggestions in this chapter

will lessen and eliminate the cravings quite quickly.

During the first few days it is common to feel worse until most of the excess mucus is cleared out. However, this usually lasts no more than four days, and the results will be worth it. The following will demonstrate my point.

'Ms M's' job had been instrumental in her landing rather ungracefully in the freezing Colorado River. She is an actress. She was to ride her unwilling horse across, when it promptly dropped her off and climbed back up the bank. Fortunately, it was her last day's shoot on the film and she flew back to LA the next day. By this time she was rather shaky, feverish, and was trying to ignore a sore throat.

She had a part in a sitcom coming up in three days and it didn't call for an actress with the 'flu. I gave her some oscillococcinum, a now world-renowned French homoepathic remedy for 'flu. Then I suggested the herb combination as outlined in this chapter, consisting mostly of cubeb berries, juniper berries and irish moss. Before bed, she also ate a small piece of toast covered with a chopped up, large clove of garlic, parsley and a little butter, then lightly toasted. I recommended a strong cup of lemon grass tea and honey with this and possibly some physical activity, though not too strenuous, to make her sweat. You may use your imagination on this one.

She only ate fruits and vegetables and vegetable broths and herb teas during this time. She felt and looked great for her next job.

Food for a week

The order of this daily food plan may be changed to suit you. After 3-6 weeks, you will feel much better and be ready to switch to the 'Maintenance Program'.

MAIN SHOPPING LIST ITEMS

Of course exclude any foods on this list that you know you are allergic to. Buy lemons, limes, tupelo or other raw honey, millet and all whole grains except wheat, e.g. barley, brown rice, oatmeal, grits and rye. All fresh fruits and vegetables that you like except those listed below under 'foods to avoid', as they are notorious for causing allergic reactions.

Especially beneficial are carrots, celery, beets, cucumbers, apricots, parsley, sprouts, turnips, yellow fruits and vegetables, green leafy vegetables, cherries, green peppers, broccoli, black currants, red cabbage, strawberries, chives, papayas, melons, fennel seeds (use them a lot for cooking fish especially), bananas, swiss chard, avocados, potatoes, yams, almonds and other raw nuts except peanuts. Sprouted grain or rye bread and crackers, garlic, cloves, apples, dates, mint tea, lemon grass tea, goat's cheese, psyllium husks, bee pollen and egg yolks.

The Diet

On arising   Fresh juice of ½ lemon or lime in 240 ml (8 fl. oz) pure warm water with ½ teaspoon tupelo or other honey (optional).

Breakfast   Millet or oatmeal or fresh fruit. Almond milk may be used here or as a snack.

Mid morning   120 ml (4 fl. oz) carrot juice and celery juice with ½ cup of water. If not available, use a fresh juice you like.

Lunch

Fresh raw vegetable and sprout salad of your choice with almond or olive oil, apple cider vinegar and herb dressing or twice a week, white fish and salad with fennel, dry or fresh. Rye crackers with a little raw butter.

Mid afternoon

120 ml (4 fl. oz) carrot, 60 ml (2 fl. oz) beet, 90 ml (3 fl. oz) cucumber juice. If not available, use a handful of almonds, or a piece of fruit in season.

Dinner

Steamed vegetables with a baked potato or yam or sautéed or wok cooked vegetables with slivered almonds and rice and salad;

or

Vegetable soup with baked potato and or salad or salad and yam. Use a lot of garlic: 3-4 chopped cloves on a piece of sprouted grain bread or in the baked potato or cooked vegetables;

or

Whole grain wheat-free pasta with virgin olive oil and garlic and salad.

Dessert

Baked apple or pear;

or

2-4 dates sandwiched into pecans with a little mint tea;

or

Fresh fruit, at least two hours after vegetables.

Before bed One teaspoon psyllium husks mixed into grape juice.

FOODS TO AVOID

All cow's milk products (goat's products seem alright for most people), wheat, all refined foods, salt, sugar, meats, coffee, wine, beer, soft drinks, black tea, citrus, except possibly lemons and limes, tomatoes, eggplant, mushrooms, eggs, preservatives and additives.

Drink a total of 6-8 glasses of spring water between meals, not with your meals as it impairs digestion.

See the back of this book for other recipe books to add variety.

After you feel better, between 1-6 weeks usually, use the maintenance program in this book.

Healing Herbs

The following herbs have been used for centuries as expectorants (clear out mucus), and for their soothing and healing properties to the respiratory system from the sinuses to the lungs. Should you also suffer from constipation, use herbs listed under 'Detoxification' as well. They all complement each other.

Cubeb berries, juniper berries, irish moss, pleurisy root, garlic, lobelia, peppermint and lemon grass. Find an already existing combination of these herbs in the health food store, even if it varies somewhat, or buy the capsules and make up your own using these herbs in equal parts. A similar tincture would also be as good, follow given directions. Start with 1 capsule per big meal and work up to 6-9 a day according to your size and need.

Exercise and a Positive Mind Set

Begin with something if you have not already, even if it's a little walk a day. Work up to at least 20 minutes four times a week of your favourite cardiovascular exercise. Take a tissue with you in case you need it. It is common to expectorate during or right after exercise, especially when clearing out the respiratory system. More so if you were a smoker.

Add a yoga class when possible as it always includes deep breathing exercises for the lungs.

Nothing, however, beats the exercise of laughing for the lungs, heart and immune function. Get to whatever makes that happen for you. Besides, it's great for the stomach muscles.

Set a goal for something you've always dreamed of and do something towards it each day. It's amazing how much that does for a positive mind set.

If you already have severe respiratory problems or are drug dependent, see your doctor and an exercise expert for advice.

CHAPTER 5

The Kidneys
and Bladder

Some signs of imbalance

> Aching bones, gas, oversensitivity to cold, low
> energy, dizziness, cystitis, mid to low back pain,
> anemia, irregular menstruation, leaking semen,
> painful soles of feet and urinary incontinence.
> Headaches, intermittent fever, sciatica, lumbago,
> tight calves and general back pain.

The kidneys extract waste from our blood, they can
affect our energy level, influence sexual vitality and help
keep proper water balance. A hot water bottle is a must
to have in the house. Place against your mid-back when
the kidneys ache, or sit on it if you have cystitis, (bladder
infection). It soothes the worst symptoms immediately.
Then see food therapy and herbs listed below.

'Ms E' suffered from urinary incontinence. Accidents during aerobics classes could be embarrassing.
They also occurred if she laughed or sneezed. On asking
further questions she told me she would endure cystitis
about 3-4 times a year, and I noticed she had dark circles
under her eyes.

She had written her average diet down for me which prompted me to ask her if she was constipated. She said 'No, I go regularly once every four days or so'. I discussed constipation with her and suggested a combination of the detoxification chapter herbs, and the kidney/bladder herb and diet plan. Her new bathroom habits were initially quite confounding to her but she got used to them. She didn't need to wear pads anymore, or make up to cover the dark circles under her eyes.

Food for a Week

MAIN SHOPPING LIST ITEMS

Lots of pure water is essential, but don't drink it with meals. Fresh limes, in acute cases ¼ of a juicy lime in 120 ml (4 fl. oz) pure water at least six times a day between light meals for cystitis, and a hot water bottle tucked between your legs. Watermelon in season, carrots, celery, spinach and parsley — lots for making juice. All fruits you like except citrus, lime being an exception. All whole grains you like — see breakfast recipes. Bananas, pumpkin seeds, papayas. All fruits and vegetables you like except tomatoes and tomato products. Fresh horseradish to add to some favourite recipes, dulse, wakame or other sea vegetables, lentils, black beans, dates, pecans, walnuts, berries, mint tea.

Once there is no more pain, you could add fish or hormone-free poultry or meat a couple of times a week.

The Diet

On arising   Juice of ½ lime in 240 ml (8 fl. oz) pure water or watermelon juice or just eat some melon or 240 ml (8 fl. oz) carrot, 30 ml (1 fl. oz) celery, 60 ml (2 fl. oz) spinach and 30 ml (1 fl. oz) parsley juice. Drink ½ now diluted with ½ water and have the other ½ in the afternoon or evening.

Breakfast

Quarter of a watermelon or fresh fruit salad in season — no citrus or one of the steamed whole grains — see breakfast.

Mid morning

Ripe bananas or juice or handful of pumpkin seeds, ½ papaya or 240 ml (8 fl. oz) pure water with lime.

Lunch

Half hour before, a glass of pure water. Raw vegetable salad, using lots of sprouts, asparagus, parsley, watercress, cucumber, celery and all other vegetables you like except tomato. You could crumble a little goat's cheese over it and eat it with avocado. (See more recipes.) Add some horseradish to your salad dressing, if you like it hot. Add 1-2 pieces of whole grain bread or rye crackers if you like.

Mid afternoon

Same as mid morning.

Dinner

Half hour before, glass of pure water with fresh lime.

Put lots of garlic into everything you can imagine eating it in.

Brown rice and vegetables — see recipes or vegetable soup with rice and sea vegetables or potatoes or yams with steamed or sauteed vegetables. Sour cream and horse-radish on potato is great.

or

Pea or lentil or black bean soup with vegetables and salad.

Dessert   At least 1 hour later.

Dates and pecans or walnuts with mint tea or papaya and berries with yoghurt or fresh whipped cream.

FOODS TO AVOID

Meats, including fish and chicken while there is pain.

Then, if you wish, 2-3 times a week, hormone and antibiotic-free, eaten with lots of salad and/or lightly cooked vegetables.

Strong spices and condiments, especially salt, coffee, wine, soft drinks, chocolate and cocoa, black teas, additives and preservatives, sugar and salt.

Note: See the back of this book for other recipe books for further variety. After 3-6 weeks of this food plan, see the 'Maintenance Program'.

Healing Herbs

The following herbs are well known to detoxify, flush, soothe and strengthen the bladder and kidneys

Vervain — 1 capsule or cup of tea at bedtime.

Gravel root, hydrangea root and horsetail (also known as shavegrass) best known for breaking down gravel and stones. 1-3 capsules with meals, according to your size. Uva ursi for minor bladder irritations in tea form or 1-3 capsules with meals.

Juniper berries, parsley, golden seal, uva ursi, oatstraw and horsetail in combination is a good general kidney tonic.

A formula close to this is usually available at your health food store or herbalist. Otherwise buy your own ground herbs and combine in equal parts; in gelatin capsules, 1-5 with meals, according to your size. Tinctures of these herbs are good, too, and include directions.

Exercise and a Positive Mind Set

I find a minimum of 20 minutes speed walk or jog 4 times a week really 'massages' the kidney area and helps that ache. Side stretches, when properly done feel great, too. Callan Pickney, in her book *Callanetics* demonstrates some excellent ones.

'I am feeling more healthy, happy and clear each day', is a good affirmation to speed reaching your goals for health. Repeat it often during your workout and whenever you think of it during the day, as well as upon waking and before sleeping.

See the motivational books listed in the back, and read a couple of pages each night, and wake up feeling great!

If you have recently had surgery or are drug dependent, seek an expert's advice for an exercise plan.

CHAPTER 6

The Liver and
Gallbladder

Some signs of imbalance

> Arthritis, bursitis, jaundice, hepatitis, skin and
> blood pressure problems, lowered immune
> function, allergies, bruises, depression, distended
> abdomen, dizziness, eye weaknesses, indigestion,
> nausea, menstrual problems, tenderness over the
> liver, temper, impatience and ambivalence.

I received a call from Indianapolis one morning. 'Mr
P.' introduced himself saying I had worked with his
sister in LA, and she had told him about my work.
Had I worked with cirrhosis of the liver? I said no,
specifically I had not. He had been diagnosed a week
ago and had a hard time with the future treatment his
doctor had outlined for him. He felt he wanted to try
the drug-free, conservative route first. Was I willing to
try? Well, I was always willing to try. He came to LA
and began treatment. I set up times for him with me
and with a physician I knew well. The doctor took his
blood once a week and monitored his progress. We
consulted and made occasional changes in his herbs and

diet as time went on. His blood count returned to 50 per cent towards normal within six weeks. He was exercising and meditating and feeling much better but not great yet. His rapid improvement had levelled off. He seemed stuck where he was and we were all a little frustrated.

He occasionally complained of mid back pain. He commenced chiropractic treatment which relieved him of the pain enormously. His blood count that week showed another 10 per cent improvement and kept doing so until it was back to its normal range.

He was beside himself with excitement and returned to Detroit to set up a new business. I have received a Christmas card each year for the last eight and he is thriving.

The liver is a most forgiving organ. Even after doing an enormous amount of the 'dirty work' of cleaning up our blood of junk food, drink and other pollutants, it will usually regenerate if given half a chance. When it does decide it is fed up, however, we really know about it. It will let us know, often very suddenly, by manifesting any of the above mentioned diseases. A little care goes a long way, however, and the use of the following foods and herbs is usually gratefully acknowledged by the liver.

A woman I saw with arthritis became one of the best advocates and promoters of these herbs and my food plan. She is a set hairdresser for film and TV, and consequently worked mostly out of trailers set up on film locations. These trailers usually have two high steps to climb up and down, which had become excruciatingly painful for her.

Her symptoms of arthritis had started about five years before and she had mostly managed to ignore them by taking over-the-counter arthritis pain tablets.

Now it was not only impossible to ignore the pain in her hips, knees and ankles, but in her arms and hands. I met her when she was part of a shoot for a commercial at a friend's apartment. We talked, and she started treatment the next week. Her pain diminished a little each week, until two months later she was pain-free. She had also dropped about 5 kg (12 lb) in weight, which, of course, also helped.

The main difficulty she had to deal with was giving up coffee. The acidity of it alone could cause a flare-up of pain in the joints. Instead she took large flasks of linden and borage tea, both very alkaline and soothing. When not too far from a health food store she picked up fresh juices for lunch. The caterers usually provided salads, so the rest was not difficult.

Specifically for the osteo-arthritis, she took a combination of white willow, devil's claw, guiaicum, red clover blossom (anodynes, anti-inflammatories, stimulate transport of nutrients) and slippery elm for soothing and nourishing. She also took the detoxification herbs. (See detoxification chapter.) She now still uses the maintenance and prevention diet most of the time, as well as a low dose of the herbs. If she's been on vacation and totally off the diet for a long time, she goes back on the original diet strictly for a few weeks, with the herbs. She now knows how to take care of herself.

During the first four days of the detoxification it usually 'lets us have it'. Lethargy, headaches, indigestion perhaps nausea and a generally unpleasant personality are not uncommon. Warn your family and tell them that you've heard that the reward is worth it.

The gallbladder works so closely in conjunction with the liver, that the information in this chapter, will in fact aid both.

Food for a Week

A minimum of 3-6 weeks for this food plan is ideal, then see the 'Maintenance program'. Drink 4-8 glasses of pure water in between meals, not with meals as it dilutes the digestive juices.

The following foods are especially beneficial to the liver, pancreas and spleen; make them the mainstay of your diet.

MAIN SHOPPING LIST ITEMS

All fruits and vegetables, especially the cruciferous ones, e.g. broccoli, cauliflower, lettuce, onions, corn, asparagus, carrots, sweet potatoes, parsley, spinach, sprouts, cabbage, watercress, turnip greens, cucumbers, green pepper, beets, endives, artichokes. Apples, dates, grapefruit, oranges, peaches, bee pollen, pomegranate, raspberries, cranberries, olives, blackberries, sunflower seeds, strawberries, papayas, limes, gooseberries, fennel seeds, plums and raisins, yoghurt, kelp, honey, almonds, walnuts, goat's milk, pumpkin seeds and garlic. Lemons, grape juice, pineapple, celery, potatoes, bananas, millet and all whole grains, black eyed peas and beans.

The Diet

On arising   Juice of ½ a fresh lemon in un-chilled spring water;

or

⅔ grape juice with ½ water;

or

180 ml (6 fl. oz) pineapple juice, ideally fresh, diluted with ½ water;

or

180 ml (6 fl. oz) carrot, 30 ml (1 fl. oz) beet, 90 ml (3 fl. oz) celery and 30 ml (1 fl. oz) raw potato FRESH — dilute with water and drink half now and half in afternoon.

Breakfast

Fruit salad of grapes, berries and bananas with or without yoghurt;

or

Millet or oatmeal or grits or barley flakes. See breakfast recipes at back of this book.

Mid morning

Juice (see above) or 1-2 bananas or goat's milk;

or

Grapes or berries.

Lunch

Any raw vegetable salad you like. Vary the vegetables listed above and use an apple cider vinegar, virgin olive oil and herb dressing.

1-2 pieces of sprouted grain or sourdough bread is good with the salad.

Mid afternoon

Same as mid morning or a handful of almonds;

or

Apples, (eat the pips if the core is clean, they contain laetrile, an anti-carcinogen), or pumpkin seeds.

Dinner

Black eyed pea or black bean soup 2-3 times a week;

or
Steamed, sautéed or wok cooked
vegetables with brown or basmati
rice or potatoes or yams;
or
Vegetable soup with artichoke or
salad or piece of bread;
or
A whole grain pasta with virgin
olive oil, garlic and other spices and
salad.

Dessert   At least 1 hour later.
Baked apple or pear;
or
Fresh berries or fresh fruit in season
with a little raw, homemade whipping cream.

FOODS TO AVOID
Soft drinks, red meats, eggs, fish, cow's milk, sugar,
refined foods, coffee, black tea and all additives and
preservatives — read labels.

Healing Herbs

The following herbs are not only well known for easing
the abovementioned diseases, they also ease sugar
cravings, open obstructions of the liver, help to restore
normal blood composition and aid elimination.

Linden blossoms, red clover blossoms, borage,
boldo leaves, yellow dock root, burdock root,
oregon grape root, and vervain. Astragalus and

gravel root, white willow, devil's claw, guiaicum and slippery elm.

Most health food stores and herbalists carry ready made combinations containing some or all of these herbs. You could start with that or buy gelatin capsules and make up your own. Show this list to them. Tinctures including these herbs are also excellent. Work your way up to taking at least 10 000 mg of vitamin C. Take it up to bowel intolerance and then cut back a little.

Exercise and a Positive Mind Set

According to Eastern philosophy and personal and professional observations, lengthy bouts of 'junking out' cause short temper, irritability and depression or, at least, not the kinds of moods you want to spend a lot of time with. As well as returning to better nutritional habits, nothing works faster to relieve this personality trait than a good cardiovascular work-out, during or after which some positive affirmations certainly help. Diseases of the liver sometimes have to do with repressed anger. When I need to run off anger I usually affirm as I go, 'this energy I am expending takes my anger with it, I am released from my anger'. If it's still there when I get back I beat up my son's enormous toy lion — when he's not looking of course. Then, if it is still there I write a letter to the person I am angry with as soon as possible, and finish up not sending it. It is rarely necessary to repeat the procedure. Anger is a toxic and time consuming emotion, so it's well worth the effort to get rid of it.

Set a goal that will make you feel good, and do

something towards it each day. A positive mind is a healing mind — more or less. See the motivational books listed in the back and read a couple of pages before going to sleep at night.

If you have recently had surgery or are drug dependent, seek an expert's advice for an exercise plan.

CHAPTER 7

The Reproductive
Organs
and Hormones

Some signs of imbalance

> Irregular periods, PMS, including irritability,
> depression, uncontrollable crying and fears,
> headaches, cramps and edema. Menopause
> difficulties, prostate problems, infertility and sex
> drive imbalances, (lacking or excessive). Chronic
> fatigue, slow metabolism, adrenal and thyroid
> function and immune function.

The reproductive organs are often a 'dumping ground'
for an overburdened liver. This can aggravate PMS in
women and prostate problems in men. To allow the
liver to clear itself, acid producing foods should be
avoided, (see foods to avoid) as they tend to tighten
muscles and tendons, causing cramps, back pain,
digestive problems and calcium malabsorption, all
aggravating symptoms. It would be helpful to combine
the advice in the liver chapter with this one.

Once a month, the female system uses menstruation to do as much house cleaning as possible. The more toxic the body is, the more chaotic PMS symptoms can be. This is usually proven after a detoxification program, when symptoms all but disappear. Restoring proper function to these organs with natural remedies has such pleasant side effects as increasing energy, easing low back pain, and restoring hormonal balance.

'M' is a dancer. Her career was in jeopardy because she experienced increasing abdominal pain, especially during ovulation and menstruation due to cystic ovaries and one large cyst the size of an orange growing outside her uterus. The recommended surgery would lay her up for some weeks and could mean a partial hysterectomy.

She wanted to try something less drastic first, since she was only in her mid-twenties and might want to bear a child one day.

She went on the diet (eating candy bars during breaks hadn't helped her condition, they also caused constipation contributing to toxicity). We used the herbs listed below, especially cramp bark, capsicum and red raspberry leaves, 2, 3 times a day in capsule form to help regulate the intermittent bleeding; also golden seal, greater celandine, bayberry, slippery elm, hawthorne berries and astragalus to help the body break up the cysts and strengthen her immunity.

The orange-size growth grew palpably smaller during the next few weeks. Her physician, after regular ultra sound check-ups, encouraged her by reporting the cysts softening and shrinking. He was happy for her. He wasn't sure what was really doing it, but glad she was participating in her own cure. She was one of the few he came across, and he was busy enough with his other patients.

Food for a Week

The following foods are especially beneficial and gently detoxifying to the reproductive organs. Make them the bulk of your food plan. However, ALL fruits, vegetables, whole grains, nuts and seeds may be used. Also plain yoghurt is good, (add fruits and/or honey yourself). Limit meat to 2-3 times a week if you feel you need it, ideally hormone and antibiotic-free. Check your health food store or local farms.

MAIN SHOPPING LIST ITEMS
All whole grains — oatmeal, barley, rye, buckweat; use the recipe section in this book to avoid overcooking. Raw almonds and other raw nuts (not peanuts), fresh oysters, molasses, apricots, grapes, red beets, lettuce, peas, parsley, sprouts, yoghurt, kelp, cherries and blueberries.

The Diet

On arising

For the juicer: fresh juice — carrot, celery, parsley and spinach juice freshly made. Dilute with ½ water. If you'd rather not invest in a juicer buy fresh carrot juice and green mix from a juice bar or health food store. Either way drink 120 ml (4 fl. oz) of juice with 1 teaspoon of psyllium husks blended in (quickly because it gels), but it will make your trips to the bathroom much happier. If you have problems with this, a tall glass of warm purified water with the juice of ½ lemon and a little honey is good, too.

Breakfast

Millet or rye flakes or oatmeal or grits or brown rice or fresh fruit in season. See recipes. Take it with you in a thermos if you are late for work;

or

One or two soft poached or boiled eggs twice a week with toasted sprouted grain bread or sourdough rye bread or rice cakes. Use just enough juice, herb tea or water to take herbs (see below).

Mid morning

A small bunch of grapes or handful of pumpkin seeds.

Lunch

A large, raw vegetable salad, using lots of seeds, sprouts, spinach, beets and tops, raisins, carrots, watercress, parsley and other leafy greens. Add other vegetables you like.

Dressings: see recipes for varieties of dressings and salads.

Mid afternoon

A small bunch of grapes or handful of pumpkin seeds, or pear.

Dinner

Steamed or wok cooked vegetables with brown or basmati rice — see recipes;

or

Vegetable soup with brown rice using kale, leeks, beets, seaweeds and other favourite vegetables;

or

A white, small fish — steamed or grilled with salad or steamed vegetables or both with lots of lemon, garlic, thyme and fennel, for flavour and easy digestion.

Dessert   About 1 hour later if you are still hungry — low fat plain yoghurt with berries and/or a little raw or tupelo honey or molasses or dates and mint tea;

or

A baked apple or pear;

or

Fresh fruit in season.

FOODS TO AVOID

The following foods are acid forming and clog up the liver and so can irritate the reproductive system — coffee, black tea, salt, sugar, all refined foods, red meats, asparagus, mushrooms, white flour, all stimulants, alcohol or soft drinks, especially the 'diet' ones.

Note: Drink a total of 6-8 glasses of spring water a day, between meals.

See the back of this book for other recipe books for further variety.

After following this food plan for 3-6 weeks, and you are feeling like yourself again, see the maintenance program in this book.

Healing Herbs

Fennel seeds, cramp bark, borage, hawthorne berries, capsicum, garlic and red raspberry leaves, astragalus, fo-ti-tieng and damiana.

These are some of the herbs that have been used for rejuvenating reproductive organs throughout history. Their perfectly balanced calcium and mineral content helps to relax cramps, and nerves, and the many other nutrients they contain tone, nourish and cleanse. You will find these herbs in various formulas or singly in most health food stores. Start with one capsule a day of the combination or single herbs with food and slowly increase to 4-8 a day according to your size.

Tinctures of these herbs are excellent, too, if you prefer drops. Follow recommended doses.

Exercise and a Positive Mind Set

A cardiovascular exercise four times a week is essential. It shakes things up increasing blood and lymph circulation, which in turn is cleansing and helps to carry nutrients to needy areas. Yoga classes are also excellent.

Throughout the exercise and in the shower often repeat: 'My health is better every day and I am entitled to miracles'. Corny? Maybe, but why blow against the wind.

If you have had surgery or are taking drugs, please seek your health care practitioner's advice first.

CHAPTER 8

Hypoglycemia,
Diabetes
and the Pancreas

Some signs of imbalance

> Depression, irritability, blank mind, impending
> sense of doom, increased blood pressure, acne,
> exhaustion, bloating, headaches, dizziness,
> allergies, excessive perspiration, blurred vision,
> lack of energy, accident-prone, candida, schi-
> zophrenia, overweight, sugar cravings.

In 1890 the milling process of grains and the refining
process of raw sugar began, removing the very nutrients
necessary for our body to use these foods, creating all
kinds of new diseases.

The first signs of stressful effects upon the pancreas
(the main sugar metabolising organ) are mood swings
and a little dizziness, headaches (hypoglycemia). They
can progress to extreme exhaustion, especially after
meals, blackouts and diabetes. Some Westerners eat
45 kg (133 lb) of sugar per person each year. Most are
now aware that this does in fact affect their health.

The progress of these symptoms, if not too far advanced, can be reversed or at least arrested with the suggestions in this chapter.

'I think I need those borage herbs that you gave my friend for his sugar cravings', said 'J'. 'I've got the same symptoms he had and a few more for good measure. I can force myself to stay away from it most of the day, then I go to bed and get back up, throw on my sweats and head down to the 7 Eleven for a Mars bar. They know me there by now.' He also had various symptoms of yeast infection, flaky skin and deposits under his nails, amongst the usual signs of fatigue and irritability which had started to dominate his life.

It didn't take much. He enjoyed the borage in tea form, and drank it instead of coffee and soft drinks during the day and in the evening. Between it and his new diet his cravings were gone in two days, and now he knows what to do should they come back.

Food for a Week

Begin by setting yourself a goal of three days without any sugar or coffee whatsoever, including honey. Cutting back slowly, of course, is fine, too, it just takes longer. Most people experience a 1-3 day withdrawal headache either way, so plan for a lost weekend if possible. Drink 8 glasses of pure water throughout the day between meals and make sure the bowels move. Use a herbal laxative at the beginning if necessary (see herbs listed under detoxification).

After 3-5 days you will most likely feel better than you have in a long time. Stick to the program for 3-6 weeks and you will find that now you can eat an ice cream occasionally, and its downside effects will be minor.

The following foods are especially beneficial to the pancreas. Make them the bulk of your food plan. All fruits and vegetables can be used unless listed under 'Foods to avoid' below, as well as whole grains. Meats should be eaten minimally at this time, hormone and antibiotic-free. At this time, eat meat with vegetables, not bread or white rice.

MAIN SHOPPING LIST ITEMS

Sprouts, bee pollen, whole grains, raw nuts, millet, garlic, artichokes, bananas, celery, grapefruit, lettuce, lemons, onions, watermelon, watercress, green onions, blueberries, yoghurt, honeydew melons, cold pressed vegetable oils, cucumbers, apricots, sweet potatoes, spinach, turnips, yellow fruits and vegetables, brown rice, fish, egg yolks, black strap molasses, legumes, pecans, peas, lima beans, pumpkin seeds, asparagus, corn, water chestnuts, potatoes, pineapples, green peppers, kelp, green leafy vegetables, cantaloupe, apples, dates (not in the first 3 days), and radishes.

The Diet

On arising

Juice of ½ lemon in warm water;
or
120 ml (4 fl. oz) unsweetened grape juice with 120 ml (4 fl. oz) water;
or
Juice carrot, beet, celery and raw potato. Dilute with ½ water. Drink ½ now and ½ later in the afternoon. If you don't want to invest in a

juicer you could buy a juice blend close to this one from the health food store, freshly squeezed that day.

Breakfast

Eat breakfast only if you are hungry, as the juice will last you for a while. Then take some fruit with you to eat later.

Fruit salad of grapes, berries and bananas. Add yoghurt and some raw nuts if extra hungry;

or

Oatmeal or left over brown rice prepared for breakfast or any of the other cereal recipes listed in this book; they are delicious and filling.

Mid morning

1-2 ripe bananas;

or

Goat's milk (unpasteurised);

or

Fresh grapes, or berries.

Lunch

A raw vegetable salad, especially concentrating on celery, parsley, cabbage, beets, beet tops, sprouts, spinach, walnuts and apple salad is good with a vinaigrette dressing. (see recipes for other salads and dressings)

1-2 pieces of whole grain bread with a little raw butter goes well with the salad.

Mid afternoon

Juice from breakfast and/or a handful of raw almonds, or apples

	— eat the pips (if clean), or pumpkin seeds.
Dinner	See the recipe section for delicious preparations of these foods.

Black eyed pea or black bean soup twice a week;

or

Vegetable soup with miso and salad;

or

Brown rice and steamed vegetables with a little raw cheese melted over them — if you don't have an allergy to it;

or

Baked potato or yam with salad and/or steamed vegetables.

Dessert   Wait about an hour after dinner.

Low fat plain yoghurt with berries in season with 1 teaspoon black strap molasses, rice syrup, or tupelo honey;

or

Baked apple or pear;

or

Fresh fruit in season with 2 tablespoons fresh whipped cream.

FOODS TO AVOID

Soft drinks, including diet soft drinks, red meats, eggs, cow's milk, sugar, refined foods, coffee, black tea and all additives and preservatives.

Note: Drink a total of 6-8 glasses of water between meals.

See the back of this book for references to other recipe books for further variety.

After following this food plan for 3-6 weeks or after your goal has been accomplished, see the maintenance program in this book.

Healing Herbs

The following herbs seem to help even the hardiest of 'sugar cravings', including the ones that take you to a 7 Eleven in your night shirt at 2 a.m.

Borage, boldo, yellow dock. If borage alone does not help, combine the three herbs in equal parts. Put the powdered herbs in a capsule, or purchase a similar, ready-made formula from your health food store, in capsule or tincture form. Start with just one a day with a meal, and slowly work your way up to 4-6 a day according to your size. Use the recommended doses printed on tincture bottles.

Exercise and a Positive Mind Set

Cardiovascular exercise is essential, a must, irreplaceable and very, very important. It oxygenates the blood, making you feel good, and helps the healing process. At least 20 minutes 4 times a week. See your health care practitioner for guidelines.

Throughout your exercise and shower often repeat: 'Every day and in every way I am better and better —

Thank you, thank you, thank you! You know you are now getting better'. Books on positive mental attitudes are listed in the back.

If you have recently had surgery or are taking drugs, please seek professional advice.

CHAPTER 9

For the Pregnant
and
Nursing Woman

Possible pregnancy problems

Edema, exhaustion, nausea, toxemia, varicose veins, stretch marks, bleeding gums, 'losing a tooth' (an old wives' tale, yet it happens often enough), pregnancy rashes, yeast infections.

The first trimester of pregnancy for many is nausea free, and a good diet is easy to stick to. For others it is not, and any food which temporarily relieves nausea is welcome. If you are one of the latter group, which I was, you can rely on the herbs listed to make sure you are getting plenty of the nutrients necessary at this time.

The second trimester is usually the most joyful, easy time physically and mentally. Salads, vegetables and nourishing herbs are extra nutritional insurance for you and your baby.

The third trimester often brings about a drop in the food intake, due to the baby crowding the stomach and other organs. The herbs once again put our minds at rest, not only for the baby, but also in preparing us for an easier labour, and to prevent us from losing a tooth after all.

The value of herbs next becomes evident during nursing when they supply mother with much needed extra energy and baby with plenty of her milk.

Infertility is on the rise in many countries now. The reasons are varied and highly debatable. They run the gamut from a higher toxicity level in our environment, to poorer quality foods, to too much time in front of computer terminals, and so on. It is hard to know, but the closest point to home is a good place to start and would do us good anyway. The following is one example of what can happen.

'A's' biological clock was causing her and her husband great distress. They wanted a child. They had been trying for the last two years without success. Her symptoms were an irregular period, frequent exhaustion, and drastic mood changes. She was also considerably overweight.

We dealt with first things first. For two weeks she followed the detoxification program. Then we changed to the reproductive diet and herbs. We focused on the calming and nourishing herbs like cramp bark and red raspberry leaves and then added damiana, black cohosh, true unicorn and virginia snake root.

She dropped 4 kg (10 lb) in three weeks had lots of energy and only minor mood swings, but she was still not pregnant. It was time to deal with her husband's side of things. He was reluctant, but came in for her. His diet was almost entirely nutrient-free, his temper short. His sperm count, he had been told, was on the low side of normal but nothing that should prevent his wife from conceiving. We talked, and he wanted a child enough to try out the program for six weeks.

Both partners became more relaxed about the situation and their clinical love life. As well as the reproductive diet he took fennel seeds (his digestion was poor) and we added hawthorne berries (high in calcium, nourishing to the blood, heart and circulation), true unicorn, fo-ti-tieng and damiana to strengthen and balance his reproductive system and act as a mild aphrodisiac.

After four weeks of her husband joining her on the program 'A' thought she was pregnant as her periods had become regular in the last couple of months. Two weeks later she confirmed the happy news. Now one might say it probably just happened because they were more relaxed about the whole thing, it might have happened anyway. You know what? They didn't care what anyone said.

We changed to the pregnancy and nursing diet and herbs and right on time she delivered a perfectly beautiful little boy.

Food for a Week

The following is the optimum diet for most pregnant and nursing women. Some find it difficult, some easy. Most women, just sticking to it 75 per cent of the time, feel great and look great, as it tends to forestall all the possible problems listed above. Make the other 25 per cent of the diet as chemical-free and hormone-free as possible. For example, for a sweet tooth, head for the goodies made with raw or maple sugar, use ice cream made with pure ingredients, like Haagen Daz, Norgen Vaas, or from the health food store, or make it yourself. Many ice creams are full of chemicals, petroleum derivatives. When using dairy foods, try to get them raw, unpasteurised, homogenised. Use whole grains for cakes and cookies.

MAIN SHOPPING LIST ITEMS

Apples, grapefruit, oranges, carrots, celery, spinach, lemons, berries, sprouts (all kinds), seeds and nuts (all kinds except peanuts), brown rice, potatoes, yams, beans, avocados, lettuce, artichokes, garlic, dates and raisins and all other fruits and vegetables that you like, especially greens. All whole grains — oatmeal, rice, barley, rye, corn.

Small amounts of raw cheese, sour cream and yoghurt. Use goat's cheese and milk instead of cow's. Also soy milk or rice milk, raspberry leaf tea, mint tea and other herb teas. Fresh juices.

The Diet

On arising
Freshly made or purchased juices, only drink citrus juices within minutes of squeezing, past that, their nutrient content is mostly lost. Some other power-packed juices are: carrot, apple, celery and spinach, solo or in combination with each other. 30 ml (1 fl. oz) spinach is enough, it's loaded with iron and very strong. Dilute all with ½ water.

Breakfast
Alternate your favourite whole grain breakfast. (See breakfast recipes.);

or

Just eat fruit in season;
or
One or two soft boiled or poached eggs twice a week with whole grain toast or rice cakes;
or
Whole grain pancakes made with buttermilk and berries using pure maple syrup or fruit topping.

Mid morning

Raspberry leaf tea, juice, small bowl of any berries, or carrots, only if you are hungry.

Lunch

Salad of fresh, raw vegetables with avocado, sprouts, some grated raw cheese or goat's cheese, seeds and nuts if you like, with a favourite dressing. See recipes. Add one or two pieces of whole grain bread if you didn't have it at breakfast. Three or four times a week, if you like, add a white fish or turkey or other hormone-free meat, steamed, grilled or poached.

Mid afternoon

Handful of pumpkin seeds or nuts (not peanuts), if hungry.

Dinner

Basmati or brown rice with vegetables;
or
Baked potato or yam with vegetables;
or
Corn tostada or burrito with beans, guacamole, salad;

or

Vegetable soup with raw cheese and rye crackers and artichokes;

or

Fruit salad with nuts and yoghurt;

or

Rice with sea vegetables and salad;

or

Whole grain pasta with virgin olive oil and garlic and salad.

Dessert
Medjool dates sandwiched between pecan nuts;

or

Berries and fresh, raw whipped cream;

or

A baked apple with raisins;

or

Home made fruit pies;

or

Mint or raspberry leaf tea.

HELPFUL HINTS

Only eat when you are hungry. You don't have to stuff down certain amounts of foods just because you are pregnant. Your body will tell you when to eat.

If very nauseous, avoid eating when you drink and drinking when you eat.

Eat dinner early when possible to avoid discomfort at night.

Drink lots of pure water between meals. It will not make you retain water.

Avoid meat and fowl containing hormones and antibiotics.

Chew your food well, and eat slowly.

From sixth and seventh months eat smaller meals more often.

You may have noticed there is no 'milk drinking' on this diet. Contrary to outdated opinions, milk is not good for you at any time and does not provide you with calcium for your baby's bones. In fact it may prevent other foods from supplying you with calcium because it causes acid, indigestion, allergies, overweight, irritability, and gives the baby colic. There is plenty of calcium, iron, folic acid in this diet, especially when including the herbs. When well-meaning advisors pressure you to drink milk for the baby and to produce more milk, just tell them that cows don't have to do that.

AVOID
Tobacco smoke, coffee and black tea, cow's milk, chemicals and preservatives (read packages and ask for MSG free foods in restaurants), salt, refined sugar and all refined foods, alcohol (except in great moderation), all soft drinks, meats and fast foods.

Herbs for Pregnancy and Nursing

Squaw vine, golden seal, yellow dock, red raspberry leaves, borage, comfrey leaves, cramp bark.

Herbs are the most perfectly balanced and easiest food supplements of all to digest, which is especially helpful during pregnancy, due to common digestive problems at this time. Their advantage during the baby's nursing time is that there is no toxicity to pass to the infant.

Using the capsuled herbs or tablet form herbs at this time with food is the simplest, as the tea isn't the tastiest elixir in the world, and the tinctures contain minute amounts of alcohol. The safety of consuming alcohol, even in the tiniest amounts, is a hot debate right now amongst health care givers.

Cramp bark, used alone, in capsules, will relieve cramps anywhere in the body. It is also well known to help prevent premature contractions and labour.

Exercise and a Positive Mind Set

During a normal pregnancy you can continue any exercise that you are already used to doing. It is not a disease or necessarily a delicate condition. However, a pregnant woman who suddenly decides to do endurance level acrobic workouts, when before she did not know what a brisk walk was, is not wise. If you have any doubts at all, consult your midwife or obstetrician.

Take your tummy for little rests whenever possible and talk with your baby, tell him or her know how you feel. I would relax deeply a couple of times each day, tell him how much I loved him already and gave lots of thank yous to the great spirit. This is especially fun when it is followed by a swift kick from a little foot. Then I visualised the delivery of a happy, healthy baby. Not that these exercises were not later put to the test, but the joy did outweigh the moments of panic and fear. Another great time for positive programming is during and after childbirth classes.

CHAPTER 10

The Prevention

and

Maintenance Program

So, now we are in shape, and we want to stay that way. It's great not to have frequent sickness slow down our lives anymore. If we want a break, we know it's all right to go to the Bahamas without guilt, rather than go to the sickbed to avoid guilt for taking a break.

If you have used one or more of the chapters in this book because of an old problem, you will already have some sense of what your body requires to maintain its new found health. You'll feel in tune with it, and it will tell you when you've overstepped the boundary between occasionally junking out and plain old punishment. The following information will be commonsense.

For the genetically strong (the 'never sick in my life' group), who nevertheless are getting older and are experiencing a few creaks and groans, some of this information may be new and possibly surprising. Well, one can always feel even better.

Being of the first group myself, I now maintain my

health simply by using herbs to make sure my immunity stays strong, and using the maintenance diet. If the immunity stays in peak condition, then the body will pretty much take care of itself. For my clients who also live in the 'fast lane', and whose health is excellent now, this is all they use, in combination with more or less regular exercise, and meditation to reinforce positive thinking. The combination of these methods of care for ourselves also enhances our looks, one of the nice side effects.

Herbs for Prevention, Maintenance and Rejuvenation

The most important consideration is to make sure that we digest properly, not only our food, but also the herbs we use for prevention which would be otherwise wasted. If daily bathroom habits are good and our internal plumbing works, then that's fine. If it is a chronic problem, as it is for many, then use the herbs suggested in the detoxification chapter as well.

There are many herbs available for immunity, maintenance and 'that glow'. I will list many to make sure that if some are not available to you, there will be plenty of others to choose from.

HERBS
Astragalus, ganoderma, juniper berries, red clover blossoms, ginseng, coconopsis, licorice root, schizandra, ligustrum, shitake, tremella (silver tree mushroom), poria, polyporus, fo-ti-tieng, oregon grape root, boldo leaves, yellow dock, vervain, cubeb berries, watercress, horsetail.

If you can get a combination that includes juniper

berries and cubeb berries, you don't have to take any extra vitamin C as they have plenty in them. If not, and you live in a smoggy environment or with smokers, take about 5000 mg per day, staggered throughout the day with meals.

The Maintenance Diet

If remembering percentages is easy for you, then the following are good rules of thumb. Eat approximately 30 per cent whole grains or potatoes or pasta, 20 per cent vegetables, not overcooked, 20 per cent fresh, seasonal fruit, 10 per cent meats, hormone and antibiotic-free whenever possible, 10 per cent dairy foods and 10 per cent junk of your choice. If you have not done so, please read the section on herbs and nutrition for health in chapter 1 to give you important background information.

SHOPPING LIST
Legumes — lentils, peas and beans.

Grains — brown rice, rye flakes, millet, oatmeal, barley and whole grain bread.

Root vegetables — potatoes, yams, sweet potatoes, jerusalem artichokes, onions, radishes and whole grain bread.

All vegetables that you like — especially leafy greens. Don't cook English spinach, it releases too much acid. Try for one meal of 80 per cent vegetables a day.

All fresh, seasonal fruit — if you find your weight creeping up, just have fruit for dinner in the summer or vegetable soup in the winter.

Meats — when possible, avoid fatty meats, pork, and meats which are not 'free range'. Grill instead of fry.

Dairy food — when and if possible, get it raw, if this is not available, use pasteurised in small quantities or get goat's cheese or soy milk. Never give pasteurised milk to children, use soy, goat's or nutmilk (see recipes). Yoghurt is fine. For infants, of course, shopping for milk shouldn't be necessary. Mother's milk is the only perfect food at that age, followed by raw goat's milk.

Junk foods — the fun part — the store-bought ingredients for Mexican food are quite good: tortillas, for tacos, tostadas, refried beans, hot sauce, cheese, olives, sour cream.

Whipping cream for desserts with berries; ice cream: most stores have it now without chemicals and preservatives; good quality coffee and, of course, an occasional wonderful chocolate for the addict — guess who? Moderation and commonsense is the key.

AVOID
'Killer junk' like plastic spray-can desserts, a lot of soft drinks, especially the 'diet' ones that consist solely of chemicals, fast-food burgers and the like, bread that can be kneaded into a little white ball and used as a guided missile, various white cakes, and most candy and sweets.

Sample Menu for Prevention and Maintenance

On arising	Squeeze the juice of ½ a fresh lemon or lime into a tall glass of warm water and take some of your herbs with it. It's great for the skin, digestion and a wake-me-up.
Breakfast	This meal depends entirely on how you feel. If you've had a big dinner

the night before, you may not feel hungry, so don't eat. If you are late for work, take your oatmeal to work with you in a thermos, or just grab some fruit. If you still enjoy coffee, this is the time to have a good cup — not instant, with a piece of toast or a 'full breakfast' — eggs, toast, fruit. Ideally no more than twice a week for this breakfast.

Mid morning

If you are on the road a lot at this time, fruit or just juice in the car always seems the most convenient. Raw, unsalted nuts are handy, too.

Lunch

One of my favourites in the summer is a tuna or salmon salad. In the winter I put it on rye bread with a hot cup of herb tea or a hot chocolate as a treat with water and soy milk.

Fruit, yoghurt and nuts are easy to take to work.

An avocado, sprout, cheese or turkey and lettuce sandwich is another favourite, and easy to come by. The possibilities are endless, just remember to try to stick to whole ingredients and the better quality foods.

Mid afternoon

Some fresh juice or herb tea. Coffee or black tea late in the day may prevent proper sleep.

Dinner

Pick up some Chinese food without

MSG if you are in a hurry. There is a large variety of chemical and preservative-free take-aways. It is worth the initial effort of finding them.

I often resort to picking up a cooked chicken or fish at a place I trust and serve 'crudite' with it. This is a glamorous name for serving big pieces of raw vegetables like carrots, broccoli, cauliflower, cabbage, kohlrabi in a basket lined with a cloth napkin. It looks very pretty.

Large pots of soup, cooked and frozen when there was more time, come in handy in busy times with a warmed brown roll and butter.

Ready made salads are another option. Many restaurants have a take-away salad bar and garlic bread.

Just make a time one or two nights a week to have steamed vegetables, to give the body a rest.

Dessert

Is really best eaten, if at all, during the day when there is time to run it off afterwards. However, baked apples with a little ice cream or fresh berries with some fresh cream should be no problem. My favourite is strawberries, ice cream and Grand Marnier. A special treat.

Maintenance and Rejuvenating Exercise for Body, Mind and Spirit

Since time was always of the essence for me in planning anything, the exercises I settled for were running, speed walking and mountain bike riding, and, on rainy days, my Jane Fonda work out tape. That way I didn't have to drive anywhere, change clothes several times and wait for a shower at the gym. I was out of the door and away.

I barely managed to start with 10 minutes at a time after I had my son and have now worked my way up to 45 minutes, though 20-30 minutes of having the heart rate up is enough, which I am very grateful for some days.

When I know there won't be much time to meditate before flying into the day, I do it while exercising and in the shower. In fact, I find these working meditations and affirmations very effective and centering. Not to mention that the focus on the meditation and/or affirmation can override the body's protests. My quiet time meditation I often finish up doing just before sleep.

The exercise creates a higher metabolism, which in turn helps with excess weight, flushes out the skin and makes it glow, improves digestion and immunity, and improves the nervous system and general disposition. Well anyway, that's what we have to keep in mind while we are doing it and our 'lower self' is saying 'who needs this?' I just remind myself that it's great when it's over.

If you are a total novice to exercise and have health problems, it would be wise to discuss this matter professionally, but there's no getting out of it. Put all that anger and frustration into it. There's always something one can do. Enjoy!

CHAPTER 11

Eve's Easy Recipes
for 40 Days
of Detoxification

*means suitable for the first week of detoxification.

Breakfast

Left over Brown or Basmati Rice Breakfast*

Warm rice, adding a little water to avoid sticking.
Add ½-1 cup (150-250 ml) raw buttermilk or kefir.
Serve and top with fresh fruit in season (not melon),
and sprinkle with cinnamon, and a little date sugar.

Fruit and Yoghurt or Cottage Cheese Breakfast*

Use fresh fruit in season.
Plain yoghurt and/or raw cottage cheese.
Top with filberts, pecan, walnuts or almonds.
No peanuts.

A Soaked Grain and Fruit
Breakfast*

This is a highly nutritious serious breakfast, which may be kept in the refrigerator for 4-5 days and eaten each morning after having been soaked 24 hours initially.

> *According to amount you want*
> **1 part almonds**
> **3 parts rolled or whole oats**
> **1 part barley**
> **1 part rye flakes**
> **½ part sesame seeds**
> **handful of dried prunes**
> **handful of raisins**

Mix all ingredients. Add equal amount of water and let it soak 24 hours.
Eat small bowlful for breakfast, cold or heated.
This makes enough for 4 people for a week.

Melon*

Should only be used alone.

Millet*

½ cup millet
cinnamon
2 cups (500 ml) spring water
apple sauce
raw butter

Rinse millet, put in saucepan with lid. Pour on 2 cups (500 ml) water. Bring to boil, then reduce heat to low. Simmer for 20 minutes. Turn off heat. Let sit for 5 minutes or until you are ready to eat.

Eat with apple sauce, cinnamon, ½ teaspoon raw butter, blanched almonds and allowed fruit.

Oatmeal, Cream of Rye, Mixed Grain Cereal, Grits or Triticale

1 cup of one of the above
handful raisins or dates (if on diet)
½ teaspoon raw butter
papaya or strawberries

Put the cup of grain into a wide mouthed thermos. Pour on 2 cups (500 ml) of boiling water. Stir, add raisins and close thermos. Let sit for 20 minutes or so.

Eat with fruit and butter.

Tofu 'French Toast'

250 g (8 oz) tofu, soft style
**1¼ cups (320 ml) amasake or soy
   milk**
1 teaspoon pure vanilla extract
½ teaspoon cinnamon
pinch sea salt

Blend all ingredients well in blender or with egg beater. Pour into a shallow dish and chill for 30 minutes. Soak slices of your favourite whole grain bread on both sides.

Carefully place slices onto a well oiled griddle or skillet and cook.

Makes about 8

Soup Meals

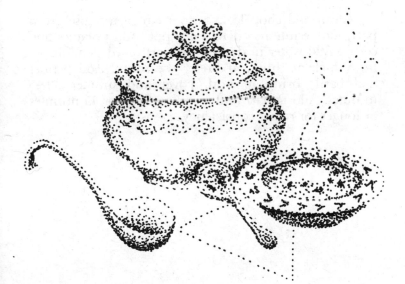

Potato and Leek Soup

2 tablespoons olive oil
2 bunches leeks (about 8-10
   medium size)
3 medium potatoes, unpeeled,
   chopped
3 stalks celery, chopped
up to 1 teaspoon pepper
½ tablespoon basil
¼ cup (60 ml) or more tamari soy
   sauce
1 cup spinach ribbon noodles
   (optional)

    Clean and chop leeks into 1 cm pieces (use green part, too). Sauté in oil in soup pot. Add potatoes and celery. Add water in desired proportion (depending on how thick or thin you prefer the soup). Add pepper and basil. Bring to boil, cover and simmer 30-45 minutes. Add tamari and noodles. Simmer 15 minutes or longer for richer consistency.

Black Bean Soup No. 1

**2 or more cups black beans
depending on thickness
2 carrots
3 sticks celery
2 onions
any other vegetables you care to
add**

Sauté with ½ water ½ oil until onions are pearly.
Add 6 cups (1.5 litres) of spring water. Bring to boil.
Add black beans that have been soaked overnight and
add 2 bay leaves, 3 garlic cloves, and 4 cloves. Turn
down heat and simmer for 1 hour. Add ½ cup (125 ml)
tamari soy sauce, red pepper, garlic and/or parsley to
taste.

Right before serving add juice of 2 lemons and
lemon slices, and dab of sour cream.

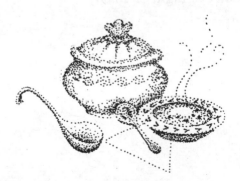

Black Bean Soup No. 2
(by Bob Denison)

Put the following ingredients into a crock pot

> 1 cup dry black beans
> ¼ cup (60 ml) olive or sesame oil
> 1 cup chopped onions (optional)
> 1 cup chopped celery
> 2 or more cloves chopped garlic
> ⅔ cup brown rice
> ¾ cup (180 ml) broth, stock or
>   water
> ⅛ teaspoon cayenne
> 1 bay leaf
> ½ teaspoon thyme
> ½ teaspoon dry mustard
> 1-2 teaspoons sea salt
> 2 peppercorns
> 2 whole cloves

Let cook overnight or all day.

Broth

Shred or chop

> **1 onion**
> **4 carrots**
> **5 celery sticks**
> **¾ bunch parsley**
> **2 zucchini**
> **3.6 litres (6 pints) pure water**

Bring water to boil and add the vegetables. Turn down heat and simmer for about 8 minutes. Strain vegetables well and drink broth, Salut! This is also called potassium or mineral broth.

A good between meal snack to warm you up in winter, soothing and strengthening for convalescence, or a two day fast.

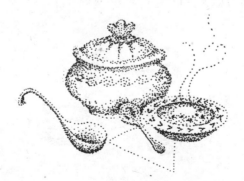

Greek Peasant Soup

1 clove garlic
4 mint leaves
small amount of sea salt
2 tablespoons olive oil
1 cup plain yoghurt
²⁄₃ cup (160 ml) buttermilk
½ large cucumber

Put first three ingredients in blender and pulverise (or use mortar and pestle). Add other ingredients and blend (if not using blender or processor, chop cucumber fine).

Refrigerate at least 1 hour.

Serves two.

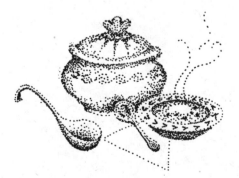

Millet Soup*

2 onions, medium size, finely
   chopped
½ cabbage head, finely chopped
2 carrots, finely chopped
6 to 8 cups (1.5-2 litres) water
1 cup millet
1 tablespoon corn oil
sea salt
2 bay leaves
pinch of thyme

Sauté the vegetables in corn oil. Roast the millet for 10 minutes. Pour vegetables and millet into boiling water. Add salt, thyme and bay leaves. Cook over low flame for 50 minutes. Keep pot covered while soup is cooking. It is the secret for better taste.

Serves 6 to 8.

Pea Soup

2 carrots
3 sticks celery
2 onions
any other vegetables you care to
add

Sauté with ½ water ½ oil until onions are pearly. Add 8 cups of spring water. Bring to boil. Add 1½ cups (190 g) of peas. Turn down heat and simmer for 1 hour. Add ½ cup (125 ml) tamari soy sauce, red pepper, garlic and/or parsley to taste.

Serves 6 to 8.

Lentil Soup

Same as above, just substitute lentils for the peas.

Vegetable Soup*

2 carrots
3 sticks celery
2 onions
add all the vegetables in your
refrigerator

Sauté with ½ water ½ oil until onions are pearly. Turn down heat and simmer for 1 hour. Add ½ cup (125 ml) tamari soy sauce, red pepper, garlic and/or parsley to taste.

Serves 6 to 8.

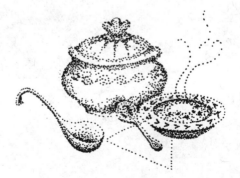

Grain and Vegetable Dishes

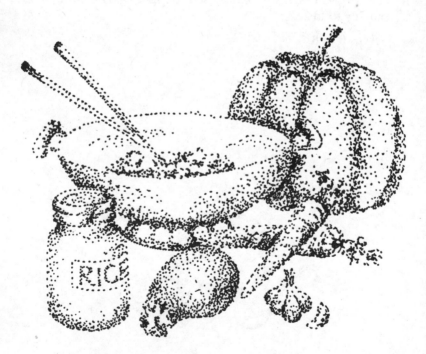

Adzuki Rice

Rice and beans are a complete protein combination.

½ cup adzuki beans
3 cups (750 ml) water
1½ teaspoons sea salt
1 cup brown rice
1 tablespoon raw butter

Soak adzuki beans in 1 cup (250 ml) water for 2 hours. Then cook slowly in same liquid for about 1 hour, until slightly tender. Bring 2 cups (500 ml) water to a boil. Add salt. Sprinkle rice into water without disturbing boiling. Add adzuki beans and their liquid. Cover and cook slowly for ¾ hour. Add butter.

If shorter cooking rice is used, cook the adzuki beans ½ hour longer before adding to rice. This side dish is also good when served cold. Toss with a little olive oil and garnish with chopped fresh herbs.

Serves 4.

Black-Eyed Peas

Soak 1 cup peas in 2 cups (500 ml)
of water for one hour

In an 8 litre saucepan sauté 3 carrots (chopped), 1 potato and a bunch of scallions in 2 tablespoons (20 ml) of fine quality olive oil and ½ cup (125 ml) of water. Add 4 cloves of peeled garlic, ½ teaspoon marjoram, savory and rosemary. Sauté for 5 minutes or until the herbs and vegetables produce a nice fragrance. Add black-eyed peas and the water they've been soaking in.

Simmer, cover and cook until beans are tender; about 40 minutes. Keep checking beans and water level. If you prefer a soup, add more water.

Note: The savory helps alleviate any gas production considerably.

Brown Rice*

Wash the rice then put 1 cup (125 g) brown rice in 2½ cups (625 ml) of hot water in a heavy two litre saucepan. Bring rice to a vigorous boil for 5 minutes — no lid. Turn heat as low as possible, cover and cook for 40 minutes.

Keep covered until you are ready to serve so rice will be fluffy.

Chestnut Rice*

Boil or roast a few chestnuts until they are tender. If you cut a slit in the rounded side of the chestnut, the way French street vendors do, they will roast quickly and the outer and inner shells will come off as easily as a peanut shell. Take the tender chestnuts — in proportions of about 1 to 5 in relation to the rice — add them to the rice, salt and water and boil the rice mixture as usual.

The chestnuts blend with the brown rice in a delectable combination of flavours.

A Wok Cooked Meal

Substitute herbs, vegetables and spices according to availability and taste.

¼ cup oil, preferably almond oil
4 cloves garlic, minced
2½ tablespoons minced ginger
1 onion, sliced
2½ cups sliced mushrooms
2 medium tomatoes, chopped
1 teaspoon diced green chilli
¼ teaspoon pepper
1 teaspoon turmeric
1 500 g (16 oz) carton tofu, drained
  and cut into small cubes
sunflower seeds
2 to 3 tablespoons soy sauce
2 avocados, peeled and sliced

Heat oil in wok, skillet or Dutch oven over medium heat.

Sauté garlic and ginger. Add and sauté onion, then zucchini. Cover and simmer 2 minutes.

Stir in mushrooms and sauté 1½ minutes. Add tomatoes and simmer 2 minutes. Blend in chilli, pepper and turmeric, cook another 2 minutes. Gently mix in tofu and 1 tablespoon sunflower seeds. Add soy sauce to taste and heat until desired temperature is reached.

Serve with avocado slices and sunflower seeds.

Serves 4 to 6.

Dolma Pilaf*

1 cup minced onion
2 cloves garlic
1 stalk celery
¼ cup sunflower
2-3 tablespoons (60 ml) olive oil
2½ cups cooked brown rice
1-2 teaspoons dried mint
juice 1 lemon
¼ cup fresh parsley, chopped
add salt and pepper

Mix together all ingredients. Bake for 20-25 minutes in oiled tray at 180°C (350°F).

Makes 6-8 servings.

Green Mix* (Dr Bieler)

7 small zucchinis
2 stalks celery
½ cup chopped parsley
sprig of mint
ground black pepper

Steam zucchini and celery until soft. Place in blender with parsley and mint and black pepper to taste. Blend and serve either hot or cold over scoop of cottage cheese (raw) if on diet.

Guacamole*

In a mixing bowl mash

1 ripe avocado

In a separate bowl mix

1 finely diced tomato with
   2½ tablespoons lemon juice
1 clove garlic, minced
½ teaspoon salt
⅛ teaspoon black pepper
⅛ teaspoon cayenne pepper
1 tablespoon diced onion

Mix with the avocado and serve with plain corn chips.

It is also delicious served with lemon juice, salt and pepper.

Hummus/Tahina*

A great dip.

> **250 g (½ lb) chick peas**
> **virgin olive oil**
> **1 cup tahini**
> **2 or 3 cloves garlic, crushed**
> **1 cup (250 ml) water**
> **2 tablespoons mint leaves, fresh or**
> **dried, finely chopped**
> **sea salt as needed or vegetable salt**

Cook the chick peas slowly in plenty of water, for about 4 hours, until they are soft and can be put through a food mill or blender. They should have the consistency of a fine paste.

Add the crushed garlic, stir in the tahini, the oil and the salt. Thin the mixture with water to make the consistency of a sturdy mayonnaise.

Stir in mint.

Lemon Beets*

Wash beets after cutting stems, leaving about 2.5 cm. Place in casserole, cover with lid and place in a 180°C (350°F) oven. 45 minutes if beets are of medium size.

Peel beets, dice, add lemon juice and raw butter and black or red pepper to taste.

Serve hot, either alone or with brown rice or steamed vegetables.

Millet Soufflé

1¾ tablespoons millet meal
½ teaspoon sea salt
⅓ cup grated parmesan cheese
⅛ teaspoon cayenne
3 beaten egg yolks
3 stiffly beaten egg whites

Mix all ingredients, folding in beaten egg whites last. Pour into oiled baking dish and cover with grated cheese. Put dish in hot water and bake in medium oven.

Serve with salad or steamed or wok cooked vegetables.

New Potatoes*

1 kg tiny new potatoes, scrubbed
boiling water
1 clove garlic, halved and crushed
¼ cup butter, melted
  (raw/unsalted)
2 tablespoons (40 ml) lemon juice
½ teaspoon paprika
1 tablespoon snipped fresh dill
  weed

Put the potatoes in the boiling water in a saucepan so that they are covered, or steam. Add the salt and garlic. Cover and simmer for 10 to 15 minutes, or until the potatoes are barely tender.

Drain the potatoes and toss with the butter, lemon juice, paprika, and dill.

Serve hot or cold.

Makes six servings.

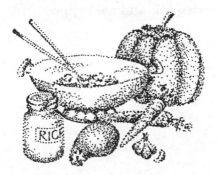

Sautéed Vegetables à la Eve*

**1 sliced yam, or potato, or banana
    squash
1 sliced zucchini
1 sliced onion or 2 leeks
bunch chopped kale and/or beet
    tops
broccoli or brussels sprouts
and/or anything you want to clear
    out of your refrigerator**

Cover bottom of saucepan with 5 ml (¼″) spring water and 1 tablespoon raw butter, olive oil or almond oil. Bring to boil and immediately start adding the vegetables. Put in the ones that take the longest first, and gradually add the others. Turn the heat to low and stir occasionally. When done to your liking, add 1 tablespoon tamari soy sauce or ½ teaspoon vege salt and a handful of sesame seeds.

Cook another minute and serve.

Tofu may also be added a couple of minutes before serving, with garlic and red pepper.

Sesame Rice*

Toast a couple of tablespoonsful of whole sesame seeds for a few minutes on the top of the stove until they turn brown. Then add them to washed brown rice and water before boiling as usual. The proportion will depend on your taste. Usually 1 tablespoon is enough for 1 cup rice.

Steamed Vegetables*

Same or similar ingredients to 'Sautéed Vegetables à la Eve', but do not cut the zucchini. It should be cooked whole so that the water inside is not lost.

Cover bottom of saucepan with 1 cm water. Place steaming basket inside it. Place vegetables in the basket.

Bring the water to a boil, then turn to ½ heat and steam for 5-10 minutes, covered.

Serve with a little raw butter and fresh lemon juice.

Tostada

Layer

> **Tortillas made from corn, lime and
> water**
> **Refried beans — make your own
> by cooking and blending your
> favourite beans or buy ready
> from health food store**
> **Lettuce, tomato and parsley,
> chopped**
> **Grated raw cheese — sprinkled on**
> **Guacamole — see recipe or just
> mash avocado with lemon and
> salsa**
> **Salsa — sugar and chemical-free**
> **Sour cream — just a dollop on top**

Yum!

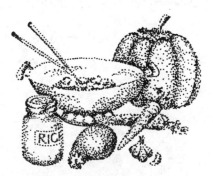

Vegetable Lasagna

1 carton whole wheat or jerusalem
    artichoke lasagna noodles
500 g (1 lb) spinach
2 cups mushrooms
1 cup grated carrots and
2 cups onion chopped
1 tablespoon cooking oil
500 ml (15 oz) can tomato sauce
approx. 180 ml (6 oz) tomato paste
½ cup chopped pitted chives
1½ teaspoons dried oregano
2 cups cream style cottage cheese
500 g (16 oz) jack cheese (sliced or
    grated)

Cook noodles and drain.

Cook spinach with no added water.

In a saucepan, sauté mushrooms, carrots and onions in oil until tender. Stir in tomato sauce and paste, olives and oregano. In greased baking dish layer all ingredients; jack cheese on top.

Vegetable Pâté

2 onions
2 cups cooked lentils
250 g (½ lb) bread
1 tablespoon oil
1 pinch of thyme, coriander, and
    nutmeg
1-2 bay leaves
½ teaspoon salt, optional
1 tablespoon tahini
1 tablespoon miso
3 tablespoons parsley, chopped
sesame seed

Sauté the onions, stirring, until they turn golden. (10 minutes medium flame). Throw in the moist bread, prepared ahead of time by soaking it in water for at least one hour and then pressing to remove the excess moisture. Keep stirring the mixture, adding water as necessary. Cook for 15 minutes over a medium flame.

Add thyme, bay leaf, coriander, nutmeg, salt and parsley. Stir 5 more minutes. Add lentils (previously cooked and blended in a mixer), and stir again. The mixture should be very heavy.

Add miso, sesame butter, and stir 5 more minutes.

Pour the whole mixture in a mould, and put in the oven. Bake 30 minutes at 180°C (350°F).

Serve cool or lukewarm.

Zucchini Casserole

2 medium zucchini
2 medium tomatoes
2 medium onions or preferably
leeks
raw monterey jack cheese

Slice zucchini and place in bottom of casserole. Slice tomatoes and cover zucchini.

Layer the onions or leeks and then the sliced monterey jack cheese.

Repeat all layers, finish with cheese on top.

Bake in 180°C (350°F) oven for 50-60 minutes, depending on how well you like your vegetables done.

Serve with baked potato and sour cream, mixed with horseradish, or brown rice.

Salads and Dressings

Carrot-Raisin Salad

¼ cup (60 ml) lemon juice
½ cup raisins
1 tablespoon chopped parsley
2 cups grated carrots
¼ teaspoon mustard
2 tablespoons mayonnaise
salt and pepper

Squeeze lemons and soak raisins in the juice. While the raisins are soaking, chop the fresh parsley and grate the carrots.

As soon as the carrots are grated, mix in the lemon juice and raisins to prevent discolouration. Add mustard, mayonnaise, salt, and freshly ground pepper. Serves two as a main luncheon dish, or four as a side salad.

Cold Lentil Salad

2 medium onions, chopped
2 cloves garlic, chopped
4 tablespoons (80 ml) olive oil
    (preferably cold pressed oil)
2 cups dry lentils
4 whole cloves
2 bay leaves
salt and pepper to taste
water to cover

Sauté onion and garlic in olive oil until transparent. Add remaining ingredients and simmer until lentils are just cooked — do not overcook. Drain, remove cloves and bay leaf, and cool. Then toss lentils in 7 tablespoons (140 ml) olive oil (preferably cold pressed oil), and 3 tablespoons (60 ml) vinegar.

Dressing for Lentils

½ cup Italian parsley, chopped
1 large onion, chopped
1 tablespoon mustard
juice of 1 lemon
salt and pepper
olive oil (preferably cold pressed
    oil)

Mix ingredients, except for olive oil. Slowly add oil until dressing thickens. Add to lentils and mix well. Garnish with watercress and tomato wedges.

Greek Salad

Dressing

> **2 cups (500 ml) olive oil**
> **½ cup (125 ml) lemon juice**
> **½ cup fresh parsley**
> **¼ teaspoon black pepper (freshly ground)**
> **¼ teaspoon salt**

Blend this and pour over one small red onion (or 1 cup onion) sliced very thinly in moon crescents. Let stand covered while the salad is being prepared.

In a wooden bowl rubbed with fresh garlic, arrange the following

> **500 g (1 lb) crisp raw spinach (English)**
> **2 ripe tomatoes, sliced in wedges**
> **6-8 Greek olives**
> **½ cup (60 g) feta cheese**

Pour dressing over salad and toss before serving.

Cooked Green Bean and Cauliflower Salad

Break into flowerettes and steam for 5 minutes

1 head cauliflower

Slice or cut in half and steam for 3 minutes

500 g (1 lb) fresh green beans

While the above vegetables are steaming mix

> **½ cup (125 ml) olive oil**
> **1 cup freshly grated**
> **parmesan cheese**
> **⅛ teaspoon fresh black pepper**
> **1½ tablespoons tarragon (optional)**
> **1 cup diced red onion**
> **½ teaspoon salt**
> **1 crushed garlic clove (optional)**

While the vegetables are still hot, mix gently together with the dressing, garnish with red radish slices and/or ripe olives and serve hot or cold.

The Salad as a Meal

1 cup finely grated carrots
1 cup whole wheat bread crumbs
1 cup grated sharp cheddar cheese
½ cup sunflower seeds
1 cup diced celery
1 cup chopped parsley
1 cup diced onions
½ cup raisins, optional

Toss together in a bowl and dress with a light herb dressing or

½ cup (125 ml) safflower oil
1 tablespoon tamari
1 tablespoon honey
2 tablespoons lemon juice
2 teaspoons basil
1 teaspoon sage
1 teaspoon kelp

Chill salad for 30 minutes and serve on a crisp leaf of romain or roll this as a stuffing into a romain leaf or pita bread and serve as a summer sandwich.

Pesto*

6 cups loosely packed basil
½ cup loosely packed parsley
½ cup pine nuts
¼ cup crushed garlic
¾ cup (200 ml) olive oil
¼ teaspoon crushed hot red pepper
flakes

Put basil, parsley, nuts, garlic in food processor. Start blending them gradually adding oil through funnel. Add red pepper and blend.

Serve on spinach pasta — add 2 tablespoons (40 ml) water from pesto water to ½ cup (125 ml) of pesto when served.

Once small amounts of cheese are back in your diet, freshly grated parmesan cheese may be added.

Salad à la Eve*

½ head of romain or endive lettuce
½ bunch watercress
¼ bunch parsley
about 10 leaves of dandelion when
    available
dry and chopped small

Grate

¼ cube raw sharp cheddar cheese
¼ head cabbage
2 medium carrots
jicama cubed, when available, or
    kohlrabi

Add to greens, then add

sprouts
chopped dates or raisins
pumpkin seeds
almonds and/or walnuts

Serve with cornbread, baked potato or sour dough
rye bread. It's a meal.

Serves about 6 people.

Salad Dressing*

**1 cup (250 ml) almond, olive,
  sesame or safflower oil
¼ cup (60 ml) fresh lemon juice or
  apple cider vinegar
dill, red pepper, garlic (fresh),
  thyme or similar herbs**

Stir together, refrigerate what you don't use.

Spinach Salad*

**1 bunch English spinach
2 green apples
pine nuts or walnuts**

Wash and chop spinach, cube green apples, toss and serve with the dressing and nuts. Dill weed can be delicious in this, too.

Dessert

The Ultimate Almond Biscuit*

3 cups (375 g) almonds
¼-½ cup (60-125 ml) apple juice
juice of 1 orange
1 teaspoon vanilla
½ teaspoon cinnamon
1 cup (250 ml) yinnie syrup or
barley malt
½ teaspoon sea salt

Grind almonds in a blender, a few at a time, to make a meal.

Add enough apple juce to make a smooth paste. Combine almond paste with remaining ingredients. Drop onto a well oiled baking sheet. Press lightly with a fork.

Bake on a high rack in a preheated oven at 160°C (325°F) for 10 minutes or just until they are golden. Watch closely — this biscuit may burn quickly.

Yields 1½ dozen

Apple Crunch*

Peel and thinly slice 10 apples. Place in a baking dish 5 cm deep. Pour on top ½ cup (125 ml) apple juice mixed with cinnamon. In a bowl mix together 1 cup whole wheat flour, 1 cup unbleached white flour, ½ teaspoon salt, ½ cup (125 ml) oil. Mix well and add ⅓ cup (85 ml) apple juice. Work all the ingredients together until the mixture is crumbly. Sprinkle over apples and let stand ½ hour.

Bake in oven at 200°C (400°F) until apples are soft and juicy, and top is beginning to brown.

Apple Delight*

Peel and slice 5 apples into quarters. Bring to a boil, 1 cup (250 ml) of water, add 2 tablespoons raisins, a drop of vanilla, and grated lemon rind. Then add apples. Cover and cook for 10 minutes over a high flame. Do not break apples.

Served cool this is most delicious.

Apple Sherbert*

2 apples, cored and chopped
2 oranges, peeled and seeded
¼ cup honey
1 large ripe banana, sliced

Put all ingredients in a blender and blend until smooth. Pour fruit mixture into an ice cream tray and store in freezer.

Sherbert can also be made by pouring the mixture into ice cube trays and freezing. When frozen, turn on the blender and add the frozen cubes one by one. Blend until creamy and serve at once in chilled sherbert glasses.

Makes about 1 litre.

Baked Apple*

The baked apple — with or without a pie-crust overcoat — is a staple dessert in the macrobiotic and other health regimes. The smaller and redder the apples, the better. A tired-looking cooking apple is apt to produce better results than its shining gorgeous cousin covered with cellophane and full of chemicals.

Remove the core from the apple, from the top — where the stem is, taking care not to pierce the bottom. Remove the seeds and core. Fill the apple with one of these:

a mixture of tahini, sesame butter and salt (very little) dried raisins

a mixture of salt and mint leaves, dried or fresh

a mixture of grated orange rind and cinnamon

Bake in a medium oven for 30 or 40 minutes until done.

Banana Ice Cream*

Freeze peeled bananas. Put through strong juicer. Other frozen fruits are good like this, too.

Dried Fruit*

A piece of dried papaya, pineapple or mango.
Unsweetened, unsulphured.

Fruit and Yoghurt or Cottage Cheese Dessert*

Use fresh fruit in season.
Plain yoghurt and/or raw cottage cheese.
Top with filberts, pecans, walnuts or almonds.

Pecan and Date Sandwich*

Sandwich dates (preferably med-jool) in between two pecan halves.
Serve with mint tea.

Sprouted Sunflower Cookies*

> **2 cups sprouted sunflower seeds**
> **½ cup raisins**
> **6 soft dates**
> **½ cup nut butter**
> **1 teaspoon ground orange peel**

Place on a wooden board and chop the first 3 ingredients. Add orange peel and enough nut butter to make mixture hold together. Form into balls and/ or other creative shapes, or form one large block and refrigerate.

When cold, cut into cookie shapes.

127

Pumpkin Candy*

1 cup pumpkin seeds, ground
½ cup grated fresh pumpkin
½ cup dates
½ cup shredded coconut

Combine first 3 ingredients and stir until well blended. Shape into small balls and roll in shredded coconut. Refrigerate until ready to serve.

Makes about 18 balls.

Drinks

Almond Milk or Cashew Milk*

1 cup almonds/cashews
2-4 cups (500-1000 ml) water
   (pure water)

Blend almonds with small amount of water, then add additional water to desired thickness. A little water will give you almond butter, more will give you almond cream and still more will give you almond milk.
Follow the same procedure for cashew milk.

Almond-Peach Shake*

2 cups (500 ml) water
2 ripe peaches
1 cup (250 ml) ice, crushed
1 tablespoon honey or pure malt
   syrup
12 almonds

Blend in the blender and serve fresh.

Apricot Drink*

2 cups dried apricots
¼ cup honey
4 cups (1 litre) water

Soak apricots in honey-water overnight. Pour plumped apricots and soaking water into a blender and blend until smooth.

Makes 4 servings.

Cashew Milk*

1 cup cashews, finely ground
4 cups (1 litre) water
4 dates

Put ground cashews and water into blender and blend for one minute. Serve plain or sweeten with 4 dates.

Makes a little more than 1 litre (2 pints).

Enzyme Milk*

1 mango or pineapple
1 banana
1 papaya
½ cup (125 ml) Rejuvelac or water

Pour Rejuvelac into blender. Add banana, papaya, and mango while blender is in motion. Add more liquid, if desired.

Makes a delicious, enzyme-filled drink.

Fiesta Punch*

2.4 litres (½ gallon) hibiscus or Red
    Zinger tea, strong
2.4 litres (½ gallon) apple juice
1 lemon, thin-sliced
1 Valencia orange, thin-sliced
fresh mint leaves

Mix all together and chill.

Health Nectar Cocktail*

> ½ cup (125 ml) carrot juice
> ¼ cup (60 ml) celery stalks, juiced
> 40 ml (2 fl. oz) of wheat grass juice
>   or water
> several sprigs of parsley
> kelp to taste

Also try blending it with ½ clove garlic.

Lassi*

An East-Indian drink used to refresh the mind and body during the hot weather. It is nourishing, light and available in most Indian restaurants.

> 1 cup (250 ml) yoghurt
> 1 cup (250 ml) ice
> 1½ teaspoons honey or maple syrup
> 1½ teaspoons fresh lime juice

Blend and serve while still frothy. A sprig of fresh mint makes this simple drink a masterpiece.

Lassi may be varied with any of the fruit concentrates (grape, apple, black cherry). Simply substitute lime juice with any of these choices.

You might like to experiment with adding extracts such as vanilla or almond.

Minted Apple Flip*

2 cups (500 ml) buttermilk
2 cups (500 ml) unsweetened apple
sauce, chilled
1 medium banana, sliced
2 to 4 drops mint flavouring
teaspoon salt

Combine buttermilk, apple sauce, banana, mint flavouring and salt in blender container. Blend until smooth.

Makes 4 servings.

Yogi Tea

This is a classic Indian recipe for a delicious and healthful beverage. About half an hour is needed for preparation.

Allow 300 ml (10 fl. oz) of water for each cup of tea, making at least four cups at once. Bring the water to a boil, then add for each cup:

3 whole cloves
4 whole green cardamon pods,
cracked
4 whole black peppercorns
½ stick cinnamon

Continue to boil at least 10 to 15 minutes, (although the spices can be boiled much longer if a stronger beverage is desired). Next add

> **¼ teaspoon black or green tea for each cup**

Steep for a couple of minutes, then add

> **½ cup (125 ml) of milk per cup of tea**

Bring back to a simmer, strain and serve, adding honey to taste.

Each ingredient of this tea has a specific bodily use: the cloves are for the nervous system; cardamon for the colon; black peppercorns for blood purification; cinnamon for the bones; milk for assimilating the spices; and the black or green tea acts to blend all the ingredients.

Ginger, 5 mm (⅛″) slice per cup, use fresh or dried, can be added for extra flavour and is useful for colds, as a flu deterrent.

Recommended Reading

For Extra Recipes

Cooking with Healthful Herbs Jean Rogers, Rodale Press, Ennaus, PA (Also provides an extensive list of mail-order sources for fresh and dried herbs, seeds and seedlings).

Fit for Life H. & M. Diamond, Warner Books

The Golden Temple Vegetarian Cookbook Yohi Bhajan, Hawthorn Books, NY

Macrobiotic Cooking for Everyone E. & W. Esko, Japan Publications, Tokyo

Nu Age Child Care Book Rising Sun Christianity Publications, Massachussets and **Recipes for Longer Life** Avery Publishing Group, New Jersey
Ann Wigmore, PhD

The Vegetarian Epicure Anna Thomas, Vintage Books, Random House, NY, 1972

Herb Books and General Health

Culpepper's Complete Herbal Nicholas Culpepper, W. Foulsham & Co, London

Herb Identifier Handbook Ingrid Gabriel, Sterling Publishing, NY

How to Live Longer and Feel Better Linus Pauling, W. H. Freeman & Co, NY

How to Raise a Healthy Child in spite of your Doctor R. Mendelsohn, M.D., Contemporary Books, Chicago
Available from: National Health Federation
PO Box 688, Monrovia, Ca. 91017 USA
or call 818/357 2181

Potters New Encyclopacdia of Medicinal Herbs and Preparations R. W. Wren, Harper & Row, New York

School of Natural Healing Dr John R. Christopher, Biworld Publishers, Proud, Utah

Motivational Books

Better and Better Ove Sehested and Burt Goldman, Uranus Publishing Co, Woodland Hills, CA

Creative Visualisation Shakti Gawain, Whatever Publishing, CA

Dynamic Laws of Prosperity Ponder, Unity Books, Unity Village, MO

Think and Grow Rich Napoleon Hill, Fawcett Crest, NY, Ballantyne

Unlimited Power Anthony Robbins, Simon & Schuster

You Can Work Your Own Miracles Napoleon Hill, Fawcett Goldmedal, Ballantyne

And any others that appeal to you in your book store.

Bibliography

Acupressure Way of Health Iona Teeguarden, Japan Publications Inc., Tokyo, Japan

Acupressure Weight Loss Program, Dr Frank R. Bahr, Ballantine Books, New York

Advanced Treatise in Herbology, Dr E. Shook, CSA Printing & Bindery, Lakemont, Georgia

Anatomical Charts of the Acupuncture Points and 14 Meridians, Chinese Traditional Medical College of Shanghai, Shanghai's People's Publishing House

Anatomy of an Illness, Norman Cousins, Bantam Books

Beads of Truth Magazines, 3HO Foundation, Los Angeles, CA

Bach Flower Remedies, Dr Phillip M. Chancellor, Keats Publishing, Inc., New Canaan, Connecticut

Childhood Diseases, Dr J. Christopher, Bi World Publishers, Inc., Utah

Culpepper's Complete Herbal, Nicholas Culpepper, W. Foulsham & Co., Ltd., London

Das Grosse Neue Gesundheits Buch, Dr Gerhard Venzmer, C. Biertelsman Verlag, German

Drink Your Troubles Away, John Lust, Benedict Lust Publications, New York

Earth Medicine, Earth Food, Michael A. Weiner, Collier McMillan Publishing, London

Elementary Treatise in Herbology, Dr E. Shook, CSA Printing & Bindery, Lakemont, Georgia

Fasting Can Save Your Life, Herbert M.Shelton, Natural Hygiene Press, Chicago

Fasting the Super Diet, Shirley Ross, Ballantine Books, New York

Feed Your Face, Dian, Dincin Buchman Redwood Burn Ltd., G.B.

Fundamentals of Yoga, Rammurti Mishra, M.D. Lancer Books, New York

Food is your Best Medicine, Henry G. Bieler, M.D., Vintage Books, Random House, New York

Herb Identifier Handbook, Ingrid Gabriel, Sterling Publishing Co., Inc., New York

Herbs and Fruit for Dieting, Ceres Esplan, Shambala Publications, Inc., Boulder, Colorado

Herbs that Heal, William A. R. Thomson, Charles Scribner's Sons, New York

How to Get Well, Paavo Airola, Health Plus Publishers, Phoenix, Arizona

Integral Yoga Hatha, Yogiraj Sri Swami Satchidananda, Holt Rinehart and Winston, New York

Living with your Body, W. Buhler, M.D., Rudolph Steiner Press, London

Medical Astrology, Omar V. Garrison, Warner, Paperback Library, New York

Natural Hormones: The Secret of Youthful Health, Carlson Wade, Parker Publishing Co., Inc., New York

Nature's Children, Juliette de Bairacli-Levy, Schocken Books, New York

Nickell's Botanical Ready Reference, J. M. Nickell, CSA Printing & Bindery, Inc., Lakemont, Georgia

No Side Effects, The Return to Herbal Medicine, La Dean Griffin, Bi World Publishers, Provo, Utah

Nutrition Almanac, Nutrition Research, Inc., McGraw Hill Book Co., New York

Old Age, Its Causes and Prevention, Sanford Bennett, The Physical Culture Publishing Co., New York

Oriental Diagnosis, Michio Kushi, Sunwheel Publications, G.B.

Potter's Encyclopaedia of Medicinal Herbs and Preparations, R. W. Wren, Harper Colophon Books, Harper & Row, New York

Rational Fasting, Prof. Arnold Ehret, Ehret Literature Publishing Co., Beaumont, California

Survival into the 21st Century, Viktoras Kulvinskas, Omangod Press, Connecticut

Symptoms, Sigmund S. Miller, Publishers of Bard, Avon

The Handbook of Alternatives to Chemical Medicine, Mildred Jackson, N.D., Terri Teague, Samuel Weiser Inc., New York

The Medical Discoveries of Edward Bach Physician, Nora Weeks, The C. W. Daniel Co., Ltd., London

The Science and Practice of Iridology, Bernard Jensen, D.C., N.D., Bernard Jensen D.C., Escondido, California

School of Natural Healing, Dr J. Christopher, Bi World Publishers, Inc., Utah

Using Plants for Healing, Nelson Coon, Rodale Press, Ennaus, PA

The Herbalist Magazines.

Index

A

Abdominal distention 14, 45
Accident prone 59
Acidophyllus 20
Acne 4, 59
Adrenal function 53
Allergies 4, 34, 45, 59
    — diet for 35-8
    — herbs for 38-9
Aloe 4, 20
Ambivalence 45
Anemia 40
Apple cider vinegar 4
Arm pain 25
Arthritis 45, 46-7
Asthma 4, 34, 59
Astragalus 54, 58, 75

B

Back pain 40
    — general 40
    — upper 34
    — mid to low 40, 46, 53
bayberry 54
Bentonite 16
Biblical references 6
Black cohosh 67
Bladder 40-44
    — exercise for 44
    — food for 41-3
    — herbs for 43-4
Blood pressure, high 15, 25, 26, 59
Bloating 59
Boldo leaves 4, 50, 64, 75
Bones, aching 40
Borage 27, 47, 50, 58, 60, 64, 72
Breathlessness 25
Bronchitis 34
Bruises 45
Burdock root 50
Bursitis 45

C

Calves, tight 40
Candida 59
Capsicum (cayenne) 27, 54, 58
Cardiovascular system 25-33
    — exercise for 31-3
    — food for 25-31
    — herbs for 27
Cascara Sagrada 4, 16, 20
Cayenne pepper 16, 20
Chamomile 8
Chest pain 25
Cholesterol 25, 26
Circulatory problems 25

BIOGRAPHY

Eve Campanelli, PhD

Eve Campanelli received her pre-college education in Germany, Australia and England.

During several bouts with cancer, between 1968-71, she began her independent study in nutrition. She moved to the US in 1972 and began her college education in Psychology at Antioch University West in 1974. In the latter part of 1975 she changed her major to Health Care and Maintenance, including science courses at Immaculate Heart and Los Angeles City College. She also began a one year internship, where she learned Applied Kinesiology and furthered her work with herbs and nutrition. She received her BA in Health Care from Antioch College in 1977.

In March 1978 she started her private practice while also working as an herbology consultant with a medical group and chiropractor.

By February 1979 she had received her Master Herbalist degree from Emerson College. From 1978-9 she added Acupressure to her studies, which she applies in her practice. She received her Nutritional Consultant's Licence in 1979.

In January 1980 she started with Ryokan College for her PhD in Holistic Medicine. Her dissertation titled 'Self-Help Reference Book', includes references re natural healing using nutrition, acupressure, herbs, juices and yoga. This book is the condensed, simplified version of that dissertation.

From late 1980-1988 she worked with her husband in their Chiropractic and Nutrition office in N. Hollywood. She teaches at schools and colleges, is an active member of the National Health Federation and received her MA in Herbology from the Rio Grande Center for Herbal Studies in 1986.

Her private practice is based on dealing with the cause of disease, taking into consideration a person's mental, physical and spiritual state, and the use of non-toxic remedies. She uses individual health programs according to the need of the person.

She is presently in private practice in Beverly Hills, California, where she lives with her husband and son.